Flight of the Loons

Table of Contents

A Letter from the President

Dear Loons Fans:

Thank you all for an incredible inaugural season at Dow Diamond. Over 324,000 fans from throughout the mid-Michigan region enjoyed Loons games with their families and friends in 2007.

The Loons and Dow Diamond are operated as non-profit corporations. Because of your overwhelming support, the Michigan Baseball Foundation will be supporting regional economic development efforts and granting funds to regional youth organizations.

We are committed to providing affordable, family entertainment and outstanding customer service in a

RIGHT: Paul Barbeau, 33, was named the president and general manager the Great Lakes Loons. Photo by Kevin Benedict

BELOW: The Great Lakes Loons take on the Lansing Lugnuts in the first game at Dow Diamond on April 13, 2007. Photo by Kevin Benedict

first class facility for years to come. We are excited that you are a member of the Loons family and look forward to seeing you at Dow Diamond in 2008.

Go Loons!

Paul Barbeau
President – General Manager

Foreword

The Great Lakes Loons first season, in baseball terms, was a hit. A Grand Slam, if you will.

With 324,564 fans attending 68 home dates this season at Dow Diamond, it's quite evident that fans in Midland, the Tri-Cities area and other nearby communities embraced this team. An average of 4,773 fans attended each game, which ranked among the top figures in the Midwest League for attendance. The team sold out 30 games.

It was the place to be this summer, that's for sure.

For many, it was a chance to watch professional baseball at an affordable price. Lawn tickets were $6, while parking near Dow Diamond cost $3. Many families took advantage of minor league baseball's family-friendly approach to business.

And for countless others, attending a Loons' baseball game was fun. Plain and simple. The game itself was one thing, but how many fans smiled at Lou E. Loon, the team's mascot? Or, how many people sang "Take me out to the ballgame" in the seventh inning or got a chuckle out of some of the on-the-field entertainment between innings or just spent some time visiting with people?

It was not only a ballgame, but a social event as well. The downtown area benefited from the Loons' presence, as more people walked the streets and visited shops and restaurants on game nights.

We'll miss the Loons this fall and winter, but fortunately for us, they'll be back next spring. We look forward to them returning to play ball, and we look forward to another fantastic summer of baseball.

We hope year two is even better than year one.

Jenny Anderson
Publisher
Midland Daily News

Midland Daily News

BELOW: Bernie Delaney, of Freeland, reacts after playing a version of the game Operation during a Loons game on July 31. On-field host Dennis Beson said contestants are supposed to use tongs to remove seven baseball-related pieces, but that Delaney pulled out the seventh piece with his hand, "so he was not a winner." Photo by Kevin Benedict

CHAPTER ONE

The Rumors are True

Big Announcement at Valley Plaza

By Dan Chalk

Those words by William S. Stavropoulos drew enthusiastic cheers from about 400 people gathered at a news conference at the Valley Plaza's Great Hall on Thursday afternoon to hear the announcement that a minor league baseball team is coming to Midland.

Stavropoulos, chairman of the board of The Dow Chemical Co., said the newly formed non-profit Michigan Baseball Foundation is close to buying a minor league team from the Midwest League, and will begin building a stadium this April that he hopes will be finished in time for the team to play in Midland in 2007.

"We are bringing a new sports venue to mid-Michigan," a beaming Stavropoulos told the crowd that included community leaders from Midland, Bay, Gladwin, Saginaw, Clare, Arenac and Genesee counties and several state and federal legislators.

The baseball atmosphere in the hall was complete with popcorn, hot dogs and bleachers. T-shirts that read "Play ball" and "2007" with two baseballs covering the zeroes were tossed out to the crowd, as is common at minor league baseball games.

The Associated Press has confirmed that the team the MBF is negotiating to purchase is the Southwest Michigan Devil Rays, a Battle Creek-based Class A affiliate of the Tampa Bay Devil Rays. But Stavropoulos could not release any details due to a confidentiality agreement.

"The sale is in the final stages," Stavropoulos said.

The Southwest Michigan Devil Rays have had nine straight winning seasons. They play a 140-game schedule, with 70 games at home.

The sale is expected to be finalized in the next few weeks, and then will require the approval of the Midwest League, Minor League Baseball and Major League Baseball.

The attempt to acquire the team has been a work in progress since last summer, Stavropoulos said.

"A whole lot of people have been working behind the scenes in the last four or five months to make this happen. The non-profit Michigan Baseball Foundation will manage and own this effort," he said.

He described minor league baseball as a $500 million industry that had an attendance of 40 million fans last year.

"Most importantly, I think baseball appeals to all walks of life and every age group, and we plan to put out a quality product that will attract people again and again," Stavropoulos said.

The cost of the stadium, being designed by Kansas City, Missouri-based HOK Sport, is projected to be between $18 million and $25 million.

Stavropoulos said it will be a multipurpose stadium that also will be able to host festivals, concerts and exhibits.

The team and the stadium will be funded in part by The Dow Chemical Co. Foundation, the Rollin M. Gerstacker Foundation, The Herbert

LEFT: The Dow Chemical Company's chairman of the board William Stavropoulos announces that "the rumors are true" - Midland plans to attract a minor league baseball team. Stavropoulos stands before a concept drawing of what Midland's new stadium would look like. Photo by Brett Marshall

H. & Grace A. Dow Foundation, the Charles J. Strosacker Foundation and Dow Corning Corp.

"We hope to attract some public money and state money," he said.

Part of Stavropoulos' motivation in bringing the team to Midland is to make the city a more attractive place for young people to live.

"We want to create a region that will attract people and retain people. And I think this sort of entertainment, this sort of venue does that," he said. "And that will attract more businesses, it will attract better people -- I think it's just something that a community like this would support and need."

Stavropoulos envisions fans coming from 30 miles away or more.

"I think the fan base will be within a 30-mile radius, and I think we're going to get them from the Thumb, we're going to get them from up north, I think we'll get them from Saginaw, Bay City, Mount Pleasant, Clare, all around," he said.

He sees the team as appealing to people of all ages.

"You go to a ballpark today, you'll see everyone from 5-year-olds to 80-year-olds. So it appeals to everyone. It's a lot of fun. Plus, minor league baseball is a lot of entertainment. It's not just baseball," he said.

He feels the business venture is worth the risk.

"There's always a risk involved, but I think if you put an affordable, quality product out there, we have the population base and the interest in this area to support a team," Stavropoulos said.

The team name will be determined with input from the community, he added. The Saginaw Spirit hockey team used the same approach in 2002 to determine the "Spirit" nickname, which was suggested by a fifth-grader in Saginaw.

The Michigan Baseball Foundation is composed of Stavropoulos; Arnold A. Allemang, senior adviser at The Dow Chemical Co.; John N. Bartos, trustee of the Charles J. Strosacker Foundation; Eric R. Gilbertson, president of Saginaw Valley State University; Michael D. Hayes, global vice president, public affairs of The Dow Chemical Co.; Dominic Monastiere, president of Chemical Bank, Bay City; and Jenée Velasquez, executive director of The Herbert H. and Grace A. Dow Foundation. ∎

ABOVE: Herbert H. and Grace A. Dow Foundation Executive Director Jenee Velasquez looks on as Saginaw Spirit owner Dick Garber tosses a T-shirt into the crowd at the end of a press conference in January 2006 announcing that a minor league baseball team was coming to Midland. Photo by Brett Marshall

A Vision About Baseball and Midland
By Chris Stevens

Decades before he became chairman of the board of The Dow Chemical Co., Bill Stavropoulos was a pretty good baseball player on Long Island.

He was a left-handed-hitting first baseman who played semiprofessional baseball, and hung around with a guy named Carl Michael Yastrzemski, who had a bit more athletic talent and ended up playing 23 seasons in a Hall of Fame career for the Boston Red Sox.

Stavropoulos and Yaz were high school chums, but Stavropoulos' idol?

"Stan Musial," Stavropoulos said of the St. Louis Cardinals' slugger. "Stan Musial was the guy. When I was 5 or 6 years old, I latched on to Stan Musial and became a big, big Cardinals' fan."

Baseball was in his blood. And, as it turns out, so was business.

They're the makings of a winning combination.

Bill Stavropoulos—most of the professional world knows him as William—is the man behind the vision to bring minor league baseball to the city of Midland.

Years ago, he wore a baseball uniform. On Thursday, Stavropoulos, 66, was in a blue business suit, announcing to the public that "the rumors are true" and that Midland is going to be home to a minor league team.

It was a sunny day, unseasonably warm for January in Michigan. Temperatures hit 50, very close to what it'd be like in April 2007 for Opening Day.

"The stars were aligned," Stavropoulos said with a smile in an one-on-one interview as he spoke about baseball coming to Midland. "It's meant to be."

His days as chairman of the Dow board are coming to an end. Interestingly, he'll be exiting the board in April, the very month that construction is set to begin on a new stadium in the downtown area.

Once the first shovel of dirt is turned, it should make the hearts of area baseball fans flutter. It certainly will for Stavropoulos.

"A lot of people have helped to make this happen," he said. "I get excited when I see other people get excited about it. I also get excited for what it can do for us as a community. I think that's really what turns me on.

"It's just wonderful to have people talk about it."

U.S. Rep. Dave Camp, R-Midland, said Stavropoulos is the one who—in sports terms—got the ball rolling.

"He is the vision behind bringing minor league baseball to Midland. Every idea starts somewhere," Camp said. "Obviously, he's assembled a great team of people, too."

Camp sees Stavropoulos thriving in his new role as leader of the foundation that will own the team.

"He's a quality individual," Camp said. "He's very smart and he's experienced. This is not a job for him. It's a passion. And, obviously, he wants to give something back to the community."

Stavropoulos' passion—and vision—is to see the Midland community flourish with the addition of a minor league team. He sees a tremendous economic impact unfolding for the area, particularly for downtown.

The organization itself will be set up as a 501(c)(3) non-profit.

"We want to see it generate excess cash to pour back into the community for youth activities," he said. "We want it to cycle. When it comes in, it goes out."

To get to the point of pursuing the purchase of a team, Stavropoulos had to go on the fast track to learn about minor league baseball. He talked to business friends. He talked to people in baseball, including the owner of the Lansing Lugnuts, a team in the Midwest League, the same league the Midland team is to play in.

"I didn't even know how to go about it," Stavropoulos said. "I talked to a lot of people and got a lot of opinions."

All of this, it turns out, began to take root last summer—roughly the same time a team in southern Michigan went up for sale. The idea itself started years before that.

"For several years I thought that minor league baseball in Midland could be a success," he said.

"In the back of my mind, I thought it'd be a wonderful thing to bring to the community.

"But I never did anything about it, because I was pretty busy," he added with a laugh. "Now that I'm (approaching) the next phase of my life, I thought a lot about what I'd want to bring to this community that would have lasting value."

Once the idea started to take shape, he went about sharing his vision privately and assembling a team to make it happen.

"Everyone I mentioned it to says it's a great idea. They're very supportive," Stavropoulos said. "The foundations have been so generous ... and Dow Chemical has been fantastic by allowing us

to buy land at a nominal value. A bunch of folks have come together to make it happen."

Stavropoulos is confident that baseball will be a hit in this area. He's seen it work in other minor league cities, and he's determined to make it work here.

He and his wife, Linda, will continue to have a home in Midland, and he plans to be a visible member of the community.

"Baseball is a vehicle for affordable entertainment," he said. "It's for all ages and for all stations of life. It becomes a better place to live. It's more fun." ■

ABOVE: Baseballs, peanuts and cleats were the decor at the January 2006 press conference announcing a minor league baseball team was coming to Midland. Photo by Brett Marshall

LEFT: "I'm just a baseball geek in Midland," Bill Kent said, proudly displaying his newly acquired T-shirt with the year of the projected opening season for Midland's minor league baseball team on the back. Kent said that the new stadium will mean he and his family will not have to travel to Detroit as often to see games. "We'll spend our time and money locally and have a better time with our kids," Kent said. Photo by Brett Marshall

The Vision Takes Shape

We Have a Name: They're the Loons!

By Dan Chalk

They came. They saw. They stood and cheered.

After more than seven months of suspense, the Michigan Baseball Foundation's minor league team has a name.

The Great Lakes Loons.

A few thousand people gathered near the Tridge and Ashman Court on Saturday and watched a big video screen at 3:10 p.m. for the unveiling of the team's name. The Great Lakes Loons will play its home opener next April 13 in a stadium being built near downtown.

The sky was overcast on Saturday, but the rain held off until about a half hour after the name was announced.

As speakers pumped out the song "Fly Away" by Lenny Kravitz, an animated bird soared across the screen, flying over the Tridge and land-

LEFT: Jenean Clarkson displays a miniature version of Lou E. Loon, one of the items to be sold at Dow Diamond. Photo by Kevin Benedict

ABOVE: "Love it love it love it," Maureen Barney-McGuire, of Gladwin, said after raising her hands in excitement as the name chosen for the Tri-City's new minor league baseball team flashed on a large portable screen behind the Ashman Court Hotel in August of 2006. Photo by Brett Marshall

ing on a nest, where the eggs hatched into baseball players. He scooped them up and deposited them onto the new baseball field, and the name "Great Lakes Loons" flashed on the screen.

Lou E. Loon, the team's red and green mascot, bounded up onto a stage, danced to the song "Louie Louie" with about 20 kids, and exhorted the crowd to make more noise. Event staff rewarded the fans by throwing "Loons" T-shirts into the crowd.

"No more secrets," said team general manager and president Paul Barbeau, who was relieved to not have to keep the secret any longer. "It's literally become kind of draining the last three or four weeks, because our preparations have been gearing up and it's been harder and harder to keep it a secret. ... I'm glad I can say 'Great Lakes Loons' when I answer the phone tomorrow."

The team that will move to Midland next year is currently called the Southwest Michigan Devil Rays and is based in Battle Creek. It is a Tampa Bay Devil Rays' Class A affiliate in the Midwest League.

Ironically, after the name was kept secret by only 50 people or fewer for the whole summer, the words "Lou E. Loon" appeared briefly on the video screen about 15 minutes before the name was unveiled — giving those who noticed it a hint of what the name would be.

"It was a technical glitch, but we'll take it," Barbeau said with a smile. "We're happy with the name, we're happy with the response today, it was a lot of fun."

Barbeau said his wife, Shauna, and their almost 2-year-old son, Peter, were in on the secret.

"Lou E. Loon's first dress rehearsal was in my basement, so Peter got a glimpse of Lou E. Loon earlier in the week," Barbeau said. "So he's already got 'Lou E.' down. That's one of the words he knows."

MBF board member Arnold Allemang said he managed to keep the team name a secret from his family.

"I haven't told anybody. (My son) Christian found out when he got here," Allemang said. "The real possibility for leaking (the secret) was at the team store at the Fashion Square Mall. But I think everybody kept it very tight."

The team store, the Loon Loft, opens today at 11:30 a.m. The team's new website (loons.com) is expected to be operating soon.

The name "Loons" was suggested by two people — 8-year-old Midlander Shawn Zebrak and Randy Trudell of Pinconning — and "Great Lakes" was added by members of the MBF, which is a non-profit foundation that will pour all of the team's profits into youth activities in the area.

"It's a traditional name — in terms of naming a team after an animal or a bird — and it's also got a lot of fun, creative, unique possibilities in terms of the name, the colors and the logo, the character of Lou E. Loon," Barbeau said.

Both parts of the name reflect Michigan, Barbeau noted.

"(The loon is) pretty common around here," he said. "We wanted to make strong connections to the region, and we think we did that both with 'Great Lakes' and with 'Loons.'

"We considered some of the other common regional identifiers, like 'Tri-Cities,' 'Mid-Michigan' and those things, but we thought 'Great Lakes' was just a little bit more special, a little bit more majestic. The first word of our name is 'Great.' That's fantastic. What a great statement to make.

"Every time someone says our name, the first thing they say about us is 'Great.' To me, that's a little bit better than 'Mid.'"

Fans can expect to see Saturday's video a lot in the future, Barbeau said.

"You'll see it a lot between now and April, and probably a lot next summer at the ballpark," he said.

ABOVE: The 47 Building, which was The Dow Chemical Co.'s original company headquarters, was built in 1916. The demolition of the building began in August of 2006 by the Bierlein Companies. "It's a part of history," said Jennifer Heronema, Dow's external communications manager for Michigan Operations. "We don't want it to go away just quietly." Photo by Layne Greene

UPPER LEFT: JoAnn Peterson, of Midland, auditions during the second public address announcer/on-field host tryouts for the Great Lakes Loons. Peterson was one of two women to audition that day. Photo by Kevin Benedict

LEFT: Bricks from The Dow Chemical Co.'s 47 Building were crushed and now have a home on the track surrounding the grass at Dow Diamond. This photo was taken in March of 2007. Photo by Kevin Benedict

At 2:30 p.m. on Saturday — a half hour before the name was scheduled to be announced — only about 50 people were gathered near the stage.

But in the next half hour, thousands streamed down from Main Street. Midland County Sheriff Jerry Nielsen estimated the crowd at 3,000 to 4,000.

"I don't think I've ever seen that many people in downtown Midland," he said.

Barbeau said he was never worried — he sees that all the time.

"In a minor league baseball game, you open your gates maybe an hour and a half before the game starts, and probably 80 percent of the crowd arrives within 15 minutes of the game starting. It's always like that," Barbeau said.

The unveiling of the team name, logo, colors and mascot was part of The Main Event, which also featured the Taste of the Tri-Cities food fair, the Battle of the Bands, a carnival midway on Main Street and an evening concert by the Larry McCray Band.

After the name was unveiled, the party

continued as Lou E. Loon led a parade of fans up the hill on Ashman Street and onto Main Street, where he perched in front of the Michigan Baseball Foundation office, posed for photos with fans, and signed autographs.

Just minutes after the unveiling, hundreds of people were lined up on Main Street to buy team merchandise from concession tables. The merchandise included baseballs, mini-bats, T-shirts, caps and banners — all with the team's red and green colors. ■

The Stadium Takes Shape

By Cheryl Wade

Although Dow Diamond Manager Greg Kigar wasn't around for the early stages of planning for the Loons' stadium, he has a feel for what William Stavropoulos, founder and president of the Michigan Baseball Foundation, had in mind from the start.

"Bill really wanted a traditional looking building" — hence the brick structure, Kigar said. "We just didn't want to build a facility that was going to look like everything else and have the same amenities, and that's why ... we have fire pits in the outfield and fireplaces in the concourse."

Battle Creek's C.O. Brown Stadium, where The West Michigan Devil Rays — the Loons' previous incarnation — played, was "older" and

had undergone piecemeal changes over the years, he said.

The Loons' new stadium has been constructed so it can be used during the off season. The bifold doors on the 15,000-square-foot concourse can be closed to house a trade show or other community events.

The new perimeter wall and landscaping between Dow Diamond and Michigan Operations was designed with the stadium in mind, said Dow spokeswoman Jennifer Heronema. For the past several years, Michigan Operations has worked to make the site more attractive and appealing for the community, she said. So Dow demolished buildings that were older and no longer economi-

ABOVE: Brian Powers of Three Rivers Corp. leads one of four morning safety meetings at Dow Diamond. Before beginning their shift, crews meet in groups of about 50 for a short review of the day's tasks and related safety issues that might arise. According to Powers, the project has had more than 240,000 work hours without injury. Photo by Jason Johns

cally viable and removed old telephone poles and obsolete fencing. Dow will continue planting grass and trees at the perimeter of Michigan Operations and within the fence line, she said.

Original plans called for flower beds around trees, but Kigar's glad that didn't come to reality even though local garden club members called and offered to help. Flowers would have needed weeding, and the stadium might have needed to hire someone to care for them. ■

ABOVE: For the groundbreaking ceremony home plate was placed where it will be located when the new baseball stadium is completed. Photo by Kevin Benedict

LEFT: Chris Larsen, welder apprentice, left, and Jeff Young, welder, both with Roese Pipeline Company Inc., work on a pipe that will reroute an existing gas line in preparation for construction of the new baseball stadium. Photo by Kevin Benedict

Project of a Lifetime

By Cheryl Wade

The last 365 days have been both exhausting and exhilarating for the hundreds of workers constructing Midland's minor league baseball stadium.

But for the paving, which will take place when the weather warms, the Dow Diamond is complete, exactly one year from the day that more than 800 people gathered at the 20-acre site for hot dogs and its official groundbreaking.

"It's been the project of a lifetime," said Three Rivers Corporation President Dan Kozakie-wicz. "Who would have ever imagined? It's going to be a landmark, not just for Midland, but for mid-Michigan."

Three Rivers has orchestrated more than 350 contractors who have topped more than 300,000 hours of work over the course of an extremely aggressive construction schedule.

Projects the size of the stadium would usually take 18 to 24 months from design to completion. But this team of workers had just

about 12.

"What motivated them was the question: How do we get there?" Kozakiewicz said. "They put together a philosophy: We are going to be successful."

And they were. Successful and safe. As opening day drew near the crew had no OSHA recordables — injuries — on the site at all, and expected that trend to continue.

Not that there weren't challenges, including a general lack of sleep and personal time during the labor-intensive project.

"I'm looking forward to opening day so I can go back to a normal life," said Ted High, Three Rivers senior project manager.

The Three Rivers workers and others have been putting in 10-hour days, six days a week, minimum.

"Every day is really busy," said General Super-intendent Mike Budek. "It keeps us hopping all day long."to hire someone to care for them. ∎

BELOW: Onlookers in an overflow crowd stand outside the tent during a groundbreaking ceremony for the new baseball stadium.
Photo by Kevin Benedict

Excitement In Town

A buzz was in the air Tuesday afternoon when members of the Michigan Baseball Foundation board of directors broke ground for the new baseball stadium that will grace the end of Main Street adjacent to The Dow Chemical Co. The groundbreaking is good news for Midland, but it is probably only the most visible sign of a renaissance taking place in this fine city.

Speaking of renaissance, the state announced this week that a Renaissance Zone at the Dow Corning Corp. Midland plant site has been created that will offer economic incentives for new development there. It will be exciting to learn what other new ventures might be coming to Midland.

Speaking of exciting, Dow Chemical announced last week that it will expand the Ashman Court Marriott Conference Hotel to include a Dow-dedicated world class training center. Officials believe the hotel will become a hotspot for idea exchange, problem solving and innovation, drawing company leaders from across the globe.

Places and events such as those described above don't occur in a vacuum, and there are many people who deserve a nod

when talking about all of the exciting opportunities that are taking place here. One, of course, is Bill Stavropoulos, recently retired chairman of the Dow board of directors, who saw the opportunity to bring a baseball team here, and did. Another is Andrew Liveris, who, since becoming president and CEO of Dow, had led a charge to improve the area's schools, recreational facilities and working opportunities. Appeals Court Judge Bill Scheme also deserves kudos for leading a group of people who are looking at bringing new opportunities to downtown and throughout Midland. The vision is to further develop the area to provide new recreational and destination opportunities for residents and guests alike.

This list could go on, but let's suffice to say it's an exciting time to live in Midland. ∎

RIGHT: Gary Tussey, of Midland, auditions during the second public address announcer/on-field host tryouts for the Great Lakes Loons at Saginaw Valley State University's Ryder Center in February of 2007. Tussey was the second of 29 people to try out that day. Photo by Kevin Benedict

ABOVE: Paul Crivac, of Three Rivers Corp., directs vehicles toward a parking lot prior to the groundbreaking ceremony for the new baseball stadium in April 2006. Photo by Kevin Benedict

TOP LEFT: Jennifer Hancock places freshly-ticketed Great Lakes Loons T-shirts, destined for sale at Dow Diamond, into a box on the third floor of Chemical Bank's Downtown Office Center in March 2007.

Photo by Kevin Benedict

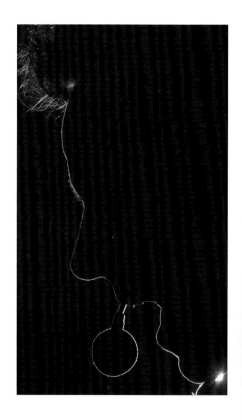

Two Pick Loons' Name
by Chris Marchand

One is a man and the other an 8-year-old boy, but both are feeling a bit Loony today.

Randy Trudell, from Pinconning, and Shawn Zebrak, a third-grade student at Adams Elementary in Midland, were named winners of the contest to name the minor league baseball team, now known as the Great Lakes Loons.

Zebrak submitted the name "Michigan Loons" while Trudell picked the nickname "Boonie Loons." Those were the only two entries referring to the nickname Loons.

As winners, Trudell and Zebrak receive season tickets to Loons' games next season as well as a Loons prize package.

The Great Lakes Loons will be flying into Midland beginning next April for their inaugural season. The long-awaited name was announced on Saturday afternoon in downtown Midland in front of an enthusiastic crowd of more than 4,000.

Zebrak came up with the name with the help of his big sister from Big Brothers/Big Sisters.

"I saw it in a book and I decided that I wanted to choose it so I picked it out," Zebrak said.

17

ABOVE: Former Northwood baseball players Ryan Stachowiak, left, Mike Henry, and current Northwood catcher Mike Koski model the Loons colors. The players wore the uniforms for away, at home and batting practice.
Photo by Jason Johns

RIGHT: Troy Mason belts out the last verse of the Star-Spangled Banner during auditions for national anthem performers at Great Lakes Loons games. Mason was one of more than 70 people to perform for a panel of judges. Photo by Jason Johns

ABOVE: Jennifer Hancock pulls tickets to be placed on Great Lakes Loons merchandise destined for sale at Dow Diamond.

Photo by Kevin Benedict

LEFT: Patrick Sheneman, 9, of Freeland, checks out a miniature baseball bat at Loon Loft in Saginaw's Fashion Square Mall while his brother Billy, 13, left, looks at apparel. The boys' grandmother, Pat Urbancik (not pictured), also of Freeland, accompanied them to the store.

Photo by Kevin Benedict

CHAPTER THREE

Key Connections

Dodgers Are the Parent Team

By Dan Chalk

Mid-Michigan and Los Angeles.

The Great Lakes and Hollywood.

The Tridge and Disneyland.

Not things you normally would group together — until today.

Shortly after 10 a.m. this morning at the Loon Loft in Fashion Square Mall, the Great Lakes Loons baseball team signed a two-year player development contract to become the Class A affiliate of the Los Angeles Dodgers. The Dodgers' Class A affiliate had been located in Columbus, Ga., and was called the Catfish.

"I've spent little time in middle America. You are the heartbeat of the country. I bring words from our owner, Frank McCourt. He is very proud to put his team here," said ex-Dodgers manager and Hall of Famer Tommy Lasorda, who was on hand at the press conference.

Loons' Team President and General Manager Paul Barbeau said the Loons discussed affiliation with a handful of teams. But in the end, he and the Loons' owners, the nonprofit Michigan Baseball Foundation, decided they couldn't go wrong with a franchise like the Dodgers.

"This isn't just any team," Barbeau said. "This is the Los Angeles Dodgers. They are one of the historic franchises in all of sports.

"They're that kind of high-profile, national brand-name, instant association with history, tradition, winning. And that's what we wanted to connect to, because I think for our franchise, it gives us instant credibility," Barbeau continued.

Michigan Baseball Foundation chairman Bill Stavropoulos is excited about the Dodgers and Loons hooking up.

"What a thrill to be starting the Great Lakes Loons' legacy with the Los Angeles Dodgers, one of the best franchises in baseball. We need each

other. The Dodgers will provide great players and community support. In return, the Dodgers will receive one of the best ballparks in minor league baseball," he said.

Barbeau said the publication Baseball America has rated the Dodgers' minor league system as the second best in baseball for each of the past three years.

Barbeau hopes the Loons and Dodgers remain affiliated for many years.

"We don't want to be a team that changes every couple of years. We want to have a long-term relationship with the Los Angeles Dodgers and have that be part of who we are," he said.

Player development contracts can be for either two years or four years. Barbeau sees the first two years as a test for the Dodgers.

"We want to make sure that the Dodgers really perform for us," he said. "And when I say 'perform,' I'm talking about players and wins and losses and those kinds of things, but primarily I'm talking about being a good partner for our franchise, being a good partner for our community, and those kinds of things."

The Dodgers have a strong local connection in Midland native Terry Collins, who is their minor league director of player development.

"This is a huge honor for me. Growing up in this area and now bringing my players here. Next April will be a big time for me," Collins said.

"Terry was very important (in the affiliation process)," Barbeau said. "He can speak to the Dodgers about the credibility of our project ... the fact that this is a very stable situation, this is a group that will do things right and Midland is a great place for players to be. He's been a great partner in this. But we look at it as being bigger than Terry. This is the Los Angeles Dodgers."

LEFT: Tommy Lasorda speaks to an audience gathered in front of Loon Loft in Saginaw's Fashion Square Mall during a press conference announcing the Great Lakes Loons as an affiliate of the Los Angeles Dodgers. Photo by Kevin Benedict

ABOVE: Los Angeles Dodgers Director of Player Development Terry Collins speaks to the media after the Dodgers announced their affiliation with the Great Lakes Loons. Collins left the organization a short time later to become a baseball manager in Japan. Former Dodgers manager Tommy Lasorda and Michigan Baseball foundation President Bill Stavropoulos are shown in the reflection. Photo by Kevin Benedict

Barbeau said the whole process of choosing a major league affiliate took about a week. Barbeau, MBF President Bill Stavropoulos and MBF Vice President Mike Hayes made the decision this past Saturday.

"Friday evening, I was at Bill's office," Barbeau said. "We had a pretty good feeling, but we had a few more questions and we wanted to give it a day.

"On Saturday, we went to the Northwood football game and then checked in with him after that and confirmed that we were still thinking the same thing, and we made the call (to the Dodgers)."

The Loons also had discussions with the Texas Rangers. Barbeau was the GM of the Spokane (Wash.) Indians, a Rangers' affiliate, before he was hired by the MBF last spring.

"We had serious conversations with the Rangers and several other teams," Barbeau said. "All of them would have been a good fit for different reasons, but when you looked at the total package, the Dodgers stood out."

The Loons will play in Midland starting next April in a stadium being built downtown. They moved to Midland at the end of the 2006 season from Battle Creek, where they were called the Southwest Michigan Devil Rays.

Southwest Michigan was affiliated with the Tampa Bay Devil Rays, but that contract expired at the end of the 2006 season, and Barbeau said Tampa Bay was interested in pursuing a team closer to Florida.

"They have some of their other affiliates in the Southeast," he said. "It was fairly apparent from the beginning that the Devil Rays and our franchise were probably going to end up parting ways."

The Dodgers, meanwhile, just ended their affiliation with the Class A Columbus (Ga.) Catfish. Fans can expect to see some of the players from that team playing for the Loons next year, Barbeau said. ■

Loons Hire Parrish

By Dan Chalk

The Great Lakes Loons scored a big victory recently by affiliating with the renowned Los Angeles Dodgers.

Now, the Dodgers have given the Loons another feather in their cap by hiring a Michigan sports icon as the team's first manager.

The Loons announced this morning that former Detroit Tigers' catcher Lance Parrish will be the first manager, a decision the Dodgers reached Friday afternoon.

Parrish, an eight-time All-Star catcher, will make his debut in the Loons' first game on April 5 in South Bend, Ind., against the South Bend Silver Hawks, and he'll make his home debut at Midland's Dow Diamond on April 13 against the Lansing Lugnuts.

"It's really the perfect fit in every way," said Paul Barbeau, Loons' president and general manager. "He spent 19 years in the majors, and from there, he spent time in Major League and Minor League coaching and managing. And on top of that, he's a name that local people know and love."

Barbeau hopes to have Parrish, 50, visit Midland some time between now and April, when the season starts.

After retiring in 1995, Parrish was the Tigers' third base coach and bullpen coach, and last season he managed the Dodgers' rookie league affiliate, the Ogden (Utah) Raptors.

"There's some element of luck involved in this," Barbeau admitted. "He was in the Dodgers' system, and he ended up managing a Dodgers' affiliate.

"But I don't want to say it's all luck. They are excited to send Lance here because they know how good the facility is, along with the community support and the front office. All those things come into play."

Parrish played for the Tigers from 1977-86 and was on their 1984 World Series championship team. He hit 324 career home runs, won three Gold Gloves, and had a .991 fielding percentage.

Parrish later played for the Philadelphia Phillies, Anaheim Angels, Seattle Mariners, Cleveland Indians, Pittsburgh Pirates and Toronto Blue Jays.

The Loons' pitching coach will be another former Tiger, Glenn Dishman, who pitched for Detroit in 1997. The Loons' hitting coach is former Dodgers' player Garey Ingram. ■

ABOVE: Lance Parrish, inaugural manager of the Great Lakes Loons, chats with Jessie Watkins, 87, of Bay City, following a press conference and interviews with media members at the Delta College Planetarium in Bay City. "I worked at the same high school that he graduated from," said Watkins, who asked Parrish to sign two newspapers, one for herself and one to send to the high school: Walnut High School in Walnut, Calif. "When I was still working, everyone was talking about Lance because he was doing so well," she said. Photo by Kevin Benedict

ALTIMORES HOST LASORDA
By Dan Chalk

What do you do when one of the most famous men in baseball comes to visit you?

When you're Frank Altimore, and the man is fellow Italian Tommy Lasorda, the answer is easy — you cook him up a big Italian dinner.

"To have the ambassador of baseball at my table was exciting — and a challenge," said Altimore, the girls' golf coach at Dow High, who is used to cooking up big spreads. "You're serving Italian food to a man who had his own line of spaghetti sauce.

"It was a wonderful evening of good wine and good conversation — and, hopefully, good food," Altimore said.

Indeed, Lasorda raved about the Wednesday night dinner that he and Altimore's brother-in-law, Terry Collins, enjoyed at the Altimores' house in Midland on the eve of a press conference announcing the Los Angeles Dodgers' affiliation with the Great Lakes Loons.

"Terry told his brother-in-law, 'Now we're really going to find out what kind of a cook you are, because we're bringing in one of the greatest food-tasters in the country, one of the greatest guys that loves to eat food,'" Lasorda said.

"So last night, by golly, this guy prepared a meal for a king," the former Dodgers' manager continued. "It was great, and I enjoyed it immensely. He made eggplant, he made pasta, he made meatballs ... and it was just outstanding. And I hadn't eaten all day, so you know one thing — that I was going to tear into it."

Lasorda and Collins — the Dodgers' director of player development — sat down to dinner with Altimore, his wife Connie, their son Greg, and Connie and Terry's father Bud Collins.

The Altimores had met Lasorda in Florida.

ABOVE: Tommy Lasorda greets those attending the press conference at Saginaw's Fashion Square Mall. Photo by Kevin Benedict

DODGERS FUN FACTS

1958 — The year that the Dodgers started playing in Los Angeles after moving from Brooklyn.

16 — The number of Dodgers who've been named Rookie of the Year, the most in Major League Baseball.

10 — The total of uniform numbers retired by the organization.

6 — Number of World Series titles won by the Dodgers.

1947 — The year that Jackie Robinson broke the color barrier in baseball (April 15, 1947).

35-35 — The current record of the Columbus Catfish, the Dodgers' Class A team in Georgia that is moving to Midland.

ABOVE: Former Dodgers manager and Hall of Famer Tommy Lasorda, bottom, chats with Saginaw Township police officers Bob Bean, left, and Mike Cohee before autographing baseballs for them as Ann Craig, director of retail operations for the Great Lakes Loons, looks on in Loon Loft. Lasorda was in town for the announcment that the Loons would be the affiliate of the Los Angeles Dodgers. Photo by Kevin Benedict

LEFT: Lance Parrish speaks during a press conference at the Delta College Planetarium in Bay City shortly after he was named manager of the Great Lakes Loons in January of 2007.

Photo by Kevin Benedict

CHAPTER FOUR

Oh, What A Ballpark!

Stadium Almost Completed

By Chris Marchand

With the Great Lakes Loons' home opener a month away, workers are feverishly putting the final touches on Dow Diamond.

About 275 workers spent Tuesday installing seats and lights. It's one of the major tasks that need to be concluded before the Loons take to the field against the Lansing Lugnuts on April 13.

"We're right where we were planning to be," said Dow Diamond Project Manager Fred Eddy. "We knew that March was going to be really hectic with the schedule. We're building a stadium in

one year. It should be at least a 1 1/2- to two-year project. We're pretty busy right now, but we're excited about where we're at."

This week, the 3,000-plus chair seats are being installed.

"By the end of next week, we expect all the seats will be installed," Eddy said. "The whole process takes about three weeks. They're about a week and a half into the process right now."

The playing surface is currently being protected by a winter growth cover. According to

---

ABOVE: Workers prepare pitching mounds in the indoor batting practice area at Dow Diamond.
Photo by Jason Johns

LEFT: A lone seat faces the third base line from the seating bowl at Dow Diamond on a drizzly day in October 2006.   Photo by Kevin Benedict

Eddy, the cover will be taken off the field by the end of next week.

"The groundskeeper has been constantly checking the grass, and he says it's in great shape," Eddy said. "He's very happy with where the grass is at right now."

Those driving past Dow Diamond will notice a large screen in centerfield. The screen is called a batter's eye and is supposed to give the batter a better view of the ball while at the plate. The screen is required at minor league parks.

Five of the six light towers have already been erected. The sixth tower was scheduled to be put up today. Once the lights are put up, workers will see that each one points at a precise angle.

"There's a lot of technology and a lot of precision that goes into putting a set of lights up," Dow Diamond Construction Manager John Swantek said. "Each lamp is aimed in a specific direction. That's so you get the maximum amount of light on the field with a minimum of spillover outside the stadium."

Work continues on a state-of-the-art speaker

system. There are about 270 speakers throughout Dow Diamond.

The next big task that faces workers is getting the mechanical and electrical devices installed, which include heating and air conditioning units. Kitchen equipment in the concession stands also needs to be installed.

Plenty of painting still needs to be done, and the suites still need to be carpeted, but most of the drywall work has been completed.

Eddy is confident that all systems will be a go come April 13.

"We may have a few things to touch up here and there," Eddy said. "We have to put another layer of asphalt on the parking lot. We probably won't get that done before opening day. Our goal is to have everything done that is required for baseball and the fans."

The parking lots will likely be paved sometime in early April, when the weather gets warm enough and the parking lot won't be used for a couple of days. Eddy thinks that the paving will be done when the Loons go on their second road trip in mid-April.

"There's a chance that we might get it done early, but a lot of things have to happen just perfect," Eddy said.

The parking lot behind rightfield can hold up to 600 vehicles, while the lot behind home plate can hold about 125. Parking costs $3. ∎

ABOVE: A layer of light green primer lines the dugouts. The dugouts eventually received a coat of dark green paint. Photo by Brett Marshall

BELOW: This aerial photograph was taken in July 2006. The future site of home plate is located at top center, represented by a concrete pad. Photo courtesy of Michigan Baseball Foundation

ABOVE: "Just housekeeping," Bryndon Budek of Midland said as he swept debris from a tunnel at Dow Diamond. Photo by Brett Marshall

BELOW: An aerial view of the stadium in August 2006. Photo by Brett Marshall

DOW PRODUCTS USED IN DOW DIAMOND

Under concrete floors and as foundation insulation
STYROFOAM(tm) Highload 40
Roof insulation
STYROFOAM(tm) Tapered DECKMATE(tm) Plus Insulation
Exterior wall vapor barrier
STYROFOAM(tm) WEATHERMATE(tm) Housewrap
Thermal and sound insulation
STYROFOAM(tm) PET Fiber Thermo-Acoustic Insulation
Plastic resin for seats
Dow UNIVAL(tm) DMDD-6200 NT 7 High Density Polyethylene Resin
Resin for play area soft surface
VORAMER(tm) MR-1160 Isocyanate
Ice melt
PELADOW(tm) Calcium Chloride Pellets
Entry plaza and other decorative decking locations
SYMMATRIX(tm) Composite Decking
Insulating crack sealer
GREAT STUFF(tm)

Fans Excited by Ballpark's Beauty

By Fred Kelly

ABOVE: "It's fantastic, first class all the way," Mike Johnson said of the new stadium as he and his son, Lance, 7, made their way up the stairs after checking out the view from behind home plate. The Johnson's were among those who braved cold weather to get a look at Dow Diamond during an open house. Photo by Brett Marshall

The weather hasn't exactly felt like spring lately, and Thursday was no exception.

It didn't matter.

After months of anticipation, even uncooperative Mother Nature couldn't keep baseball fans from flocking to Dow Diamond, home of the Great Lakes Loons, for Thursday evening's open house.

And according to many fans, the stadium has been worth the wait — and worth braving the cold and wind.

"I think it's awesome. This is just beautiful," said Midland's Bob Lanning, who has been to minor league ballparks in Grand Rapids, Lansing, and Peoria, Ill., among others. "I've never seen anything like it. It's just so much better than (other minor league ballparks I've seen). ... It looks like a major league ballpark."

Indeed, Dow Diamond — with its predominantly green color scheme, spacious concourses, gently sloping stadium seating, colorful scoreboard and scenic view — brings to mind a certain major league park in southeastern Michigan.

As Loons' President and General Manager Paul Barbeau noted, Dow Diamond certainly doesn't have the feel of a typical Class A park.

"I've been to a lot of (minor league parks) over the years, and I haven't seen anything better,"

Barbeau said. " ... The only thing that keeps this from being (like) a state-of-the-art major league ballpark is that it's a little smaller. But other than that, it's just like the nicest major league ballpark you can build."

Midland's Bill Kent seemed almost overwhelmed as he sat with two of his young daughters in seats a few rows up from the first base dugout.

"Oh, it's beautiful. I think it's great," said Kent, who has purchased a 26-game ticket package and was checking out the view from his game-day seat. "It's actually even more open than Comerica Park. You can see everything."

Although he was impressed with the stadium as a whole, Kent said he is most excited about the park's sprawling playground area just beyond the rightfield line.

"The coolest thing, honestly, is the play area out there," said Kent, a father of three. "We looked at that and thought, 'OK, that's going to be a really cool place for our (children) to play at.'"

Kent's nine-year-old daughter, Madison, couldn't have agreed more.

"It's cool. I'm going to a birthday party for one of my friends here soon, and we're going to be watching the game and playing in the play place," said Madison Kent, a third-grader at Siebert Elementary. "She's inviting a lot of people, and

we're going to have a lot of fun here."

Going to Dow Diamond won't be solely play time for Madison, though. She also intends to enjoy some baseball.

Asked what she looks forward to the most, she replied, "I'm probably going to look forward to watching their games."

Chris Brasseur is also looking forward to watching the Loons play — so much so, in fact, that he drove all the way from his home in Saginaw just to sit in his assigned seat behind home plate.

"I'm just seeing how it feels to sit here and take in this great view," said Brasseur, who sat bundled up and alone for a long time, listening to the broadcast of the Loons' season opener in South Bend and looking out over Dow Diamond.

"It's cold, but I love it," added Brasseur, a season-ticket holder. "It's everything I expected. ... I'm impressed. I've been in a few other minor league stadiums, and this is a lot better than any of the other ones I've been in." ∎

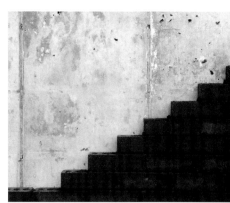

Getting the Park Ready

By Cheryl Wade

Although Dow Diamond Manager Greg Kigar wasn't around for the early stages of planning for the Loons' stadium, he has a feel for what William Stavropoulos, founder and president of the Michigan Baseball Foundation, had in mind from the start.

"Bill really wanted a traditional looking building" — hence the brick structure, Kigar said. "We just didn't want to build a facility that was going to look like everything else and have the same amenities, and that's why ... we have fire pits in the outfield and fireplaces in the concourse."

Battle Creek's C.O. Brown Stadium, where The West Michigan Devil Rays — the Loons' previous incarnation — played, was "older" and had undergone piecemeal changes over the years, he said.

The Loons' new stadium has been constructed so it can be used during the off season. The bifold doors on the 15,000-square-foot concourse can be closed to house a trade show or other community events.

The new perimeter wall and landscaping between Dow Diamond and Michigan Operations was designed with the stadium in mind, said Dow spokeswoman Jennifer Heronema. For the past several years, Michigan Operations has worked to make the site more attractive and appealing for the community, she said. So Dow demolished buildings that were older and no longer economically viable and removed old telephone poles and obsolete fencing. Dow will continue planting grass and trees at the perimeter of Michigan Operations and within the fence line, she said.

Original plans called for flower beds around trees, but Kigar's glad that didn't come to reality even though local garden club members called and offered to help. Flowers would have needed weeding, and the stadium might have needed to hire someone to care for them. ■

ABOVE: A concrete riser section is moved by crane toward the ground before installation in a seating area of the new baseball stadium. Photo by Kevin Benedict

Parrish Loves the Park

By Chris Marchand

Lance Parrish appeared in the interview room at Dow Diamond on Tuesday ready to talk a little baseball. But the big topic centered on not his players, but the players' new home.

Parrish and his players raved about the 5,200-seat Dow Diamond. The team spent Tuesday still getting settled in after arriving late Monday from their spring training site in Vero Beach, Fla.

"It's just a beautiful facility," Parrish said during a press conference Tuesday at the stadium. "It's beyond everyone in this clubhouse's wildest dreams. They're definitely going to be spoiled here this year. I'm sure it's unlike anything they've played in before. We can't wait to get going."

Player workouts and the subsequent media day were scheduled to take place on the Dow Diamond field. But heavy rain moved the festivities inside. Parrish and his players spent Tuesday taking advantage of the first-class amenities the new stadium has to offer.

"We got a chance to use the new batting cage so that was nice as well," Parrish said. "It is a very beautiful facility."

Several players expressed their impression of Dow Diamond.

"It's an awesome place, a great stadium," Loons pitcher Clayton Kershaw said. "I love it. When we got here, we didn't know that the stadium was going to be anywhere near this nice."

Pitcher Doug Brooks is from downstate Taylor and was instantly impressed by the facility.

"I actually drove in late last night," Brooks said. "I went home first and I got to see the stadium from the road and it looked pretty good. I'm excited for the season to start."

Loons pitching coach Glenn Dishman thinks that Dow Diamond could be a second home for a lot of players.

"This is nicer than a lot of big league parks," he said. "In single-A, or AA ball, guys come to the ball park as late as they can. They stay and play and then they leave as fast as they can. This will be a place where guys come, be with their teammates and hang out and enjoy their time.

"I already told my wife that if I'm not home by one or two o'clock in the morning, you know where I am. It's not at the bar, it's at the clubhouse."

Not even the cold, wet weather could put a damper on Preston Mattingly's view of the stadium. Mattingly played last year in the Gulf Coast League at Vero Beach. He says the facilities are a big upgrade.

"We played on one of the back fields so it's about 110 (degrees) every day. We played at 12 o'clock so this is a step up. I don't care if it's five degrees, I'd rather play here all day long." ∎

LEFT: In this aerial view of the stadium in August 2006, The Dow Chemical Co. is seen in the background. Photo by Brett Marshall

TOP: Workers from H & H Contracting, Jim Whitney and Bob Martin, install anchors for seats that are filling Dow Diamond. Photo by Ryan Wood

BELOW: Construction workers braved wet and cold weather to work on the new Dow Diamond. Photo by Jesse Osbourne

Lighting up the Diamond
By Dan Chalk

The Great Lakes Loons' players probably won't know what foot-candles are. But they will likely appreciate how well-lit the field is at the Loons' first home game on April 13.

Blasy Electric Inc. of Midland is one of three companies that are working together to install six light poles at Dow Diamond that will illuminate the field at standards set for AAA baseball teams, a level two notches above the Class A Loons.

Those standards call for 100 foot-candles on the infield and 70 foot-candles on the outfield. One foot-candle is the amount of light that a candle generates one foot away.

"It used to be that 100 foot-candles was the recommended lighting level for an office. Now they've scaled that back to 60," said Blasy Electric President Don Blasy by way of comparison.

"The goal is that five years down the road, we will still have 100 and 70 (for the illumination levels at Dow Diamond)," Blasy said.

The poles contain a total of 196 1,500-watt metal halide fixtures with GE lamps, operated at 480 volts.

One light pole was installed last Thursday, and the other five are scheduled to be installed today and Tuesday, Blasy said.

Blasy Electric's involvement with the project began in November and has involved thousands of man-hours in assembling the light poles.

"It's been a lot of fun," Blasy said.

Universal Sports Lighting of Atlanta, Ill., manufactured the light fixtures and designed the lighting system, and Makers Sales and Marketing of Halstrom City, Texas, designed and manufactured the poles.

Blasy Electric installs the wiring, mounts the ballast boxes and fixtures, performs the testing, and verifies the illumination levels. Bierlein Companies unloads the poles, slips them together, and installs them, assisted by McNally-Nimergood in the setting of the two largest poles.

The two "A" poles will sit on steel structure columns on the roof of the concourse. They are 95 feet long but reach about 135 feet above home plate.

The two "B" poles will sit on concrete bases on the berms behind the left-field and right-field foul lines. They are 97 feet long and reach about 116 feet above home plate.

The two "C" poles will sit on concrete bases outside the outfield concrete retaining wall, measuring 100 feet long and rising 108 feet above home plate. ∎

ABOVE: Mike Budek, general superintendent of Three Rivers Corp., fields one of the many calls from workers on site at Dow Diamond. Photo by Jason Johns

BELOW: Heath Hage, top, and Joe Anderson of Blasy Electric attach one of 48 1500-watt lights to be erected along the first base line at Dow Diamond. Photo by Jason Johns

ABOVE A cracked layer of clay conceals a layer of unfired clay bricks that line the bottom of the pitcher's mound, home plate, and the bullpen at Dow Diamond. The bricks are in place to cut down on wear and give a firm surface for support. Photo by Brett Marshall

BELOW: Lake Painting employees George Flood, left, and Josh Sauvage work on rust proofing and touching up the scoreboard at Dow Diamond. Photo by Ryan Wood

Best in their Field

The Midwest League has named the Great Lakes Loons' Dow Diamond Grounds Crew as the top Grounds Crew in the Midwest League for the 2007 season. The crew is headed by Matt McQuaid, the Head Groundskeeper for the Great Lakes Loons.

The league's managers selected Dow Diamond's crew for the award. A statement released by Midwest League President George Spelius said the Loons' Grounds Crew "demonstrated a commitment and dedication to providing a first-rate playing surface, making them a respected leader in the Sports Turf industry."

The award was based on "quality of playing surface, playability and texture of infield skin, preparation of field, condition of infield and outfield turf, quality of pitching mounds, and overall professionalism of staff."

"This is a tremendous honor for our grounds crew and for Dow Diamond," said Loons President and General Manager Paul Barbeau. "This award is a testament to Matt McQuaid and his tremendous staff for their hard work, professionalism and dedication."

ABOVE: Responsible for the oversight of construction at Dow Diamond are, clockwise from left, Mike Budek, general superintendent, Dan Kozakiewicz, president of Three Rivers Corp., John Swantek, construction manager, Fred Eddy, project manager, Ted High, project manager and Garry McKellar, site foreman. Photo by Jason Johns

BELOW: Workers from J.E. Johnson, including Dale Thornton, right, Gary Stefanski, Tim Gordon and Jason Sturgeon complete their pre-task analysis cards after a morning tailgate safety meeting at Dow Diamond. Photo by Jason Johns

LEFT: After cleaning dust from his clothes and gear, Pumford cement finisher Chris Lawmaster, of Auburn, puts in ear plugs before returning to grinding the seams of the cement walls of the new stadium's fixed seating area in September 2006. "It's pretty cool because I'm close to home. Ten minutes all summer," Lawmaster said of the convenience of the site. Photo by Brett Marshall

BELOW: Joe O'Rourke, Jr., left, of Whaley Steel Corp., and Matt Brady, of Pumford Construction, Inc., tend to cement poured in June 2006 for tunnel walls in Midland's new baseball stadium. Photo by Kevin Benedict.

ABOVE: Photographs, drawings, greeting cards and lottery tickets tacked to the wall by workers at Dow Diamond represent the many reasons for working safe. *Photo by Jason Johns*

LEFT: Ric Anderson, of Three Rivers Corp., cuts a piece of rebar at Dow Diamond in preparation for the pouring of concrete steps at the top of the seating bowl. "It's a new experience," Anderson said of working on the stadium. *Photo by Kevin Benedict*

BELOW: Mark Wilcox, right, pulls a chalk line from Kevin Kamuda, left, while the employees of Sport Surface Specialties, LLC, of East Aurora, New York, work in the playground area at Dow Diamond in March 2007. *Photo by Kevin Benedict*

CHAPTER FIVE

Spring Training

Parrish Talks About Spring Training
By Chris Marchand

Lance Parrish has been upbeat for the last few days.

On Sunday, he joked with a few old friends, signed autographs for exuberant fans. He also found time to manage a baseball team which is going well by all accounts.

If there's any pressure to managing a baseball team coming to a new town, Parrish certainly isn't feeling it.

With the Great Lakes Loons set to open their inaugural season in just over a week, Parrish likes the prospects of his team.

"Things are going well," he said. "Our teams are starting to shape up. Early in camp, some players are everywhere, but we're starting to zero in on the players (going to Midland).

"It's going to be an exciting team," he added. "I like the way things are shaping up and I think we're going to be very competitive and I'm excited about that."

The Loons proved that on Tuesday afternoon. Trailing 3-1 to the New York Mets, they rallied with three runs in the ninth inning to post a 7-4 victory.

The team also has two wins in three games against the Dodgers' Upper Class A team San Bernardino.

With four days left of spring training, Parrish's club is just about finalized.

"Most of the guys that we have right now will be going to Midland," Parrish said. "The good thing is that I had most of these guys last year in

ABOVE: Parker Brooks, left, repeatedly sits baseballs atop the tee for Tommy Giles before switching off and batting himself. The pair were competing to see who could hit the ball into a hole in the netting use by the mechanical pitching machine. Brooks came away the victor. Photo by Brett Marshall

LEFT: Lying in the midday sun, Dodgers minor league outfielder Tommy Giles relaxes while a team trainer stretches his legs after running. Photo by Brett Marshall

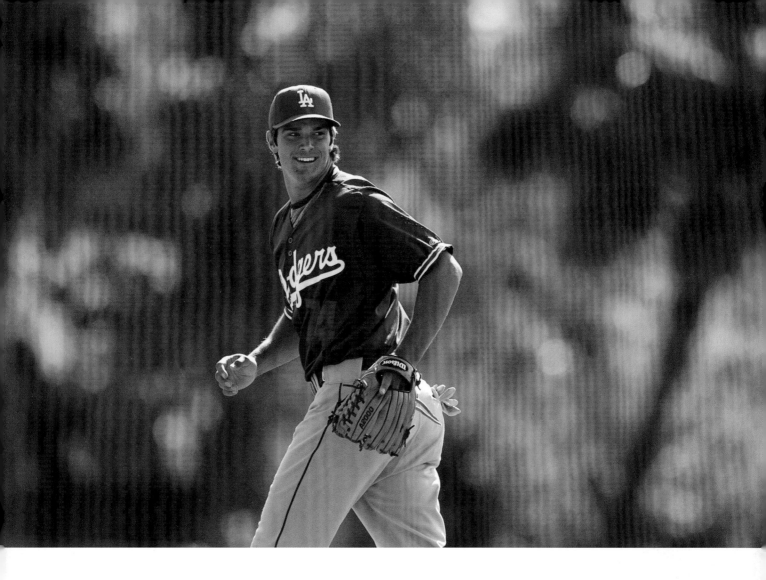

Odgen. There could be a few additions to that, but I think we have a pretty solid group. They've blended well together. They like each other."

The key now is to avoid any injuries that could force players to miss a considerable length of time. Parrish will also spend the final days in Florida fine-tuning his players.

"It's basically just a matter of getting these guys working well together," Parrish said. "They know how to execute, they know how to play the game. We go over these plays a million times so they know where they're supposed to be in any given situation."

The Loons' roster is likely to include two first-round draft picks - pitcher Clayton Kershaw and shortstop Preston Mattingly.

Kershaw, the seventh overall pick in the 2006 draft, was nearly unhittable as a senior in 2005 at Highland Park High School in Texas. He was just as impressive in Rookie League play at Odgen. He struck out 54 in 37 innings of work.

"He's pretty special," Parrish said. "He's really well-thought of in this organization. Obviously he was our No. 1 draft pick in this organization

and everyone is really excited about him. We will have him to start the season, but if he pitches the way everyone expects him to, I don't know how long we'll be able to hang on to him. If anyone is on a fast track in this organization, it will probably be him."

Kershaw is the second-highest rated prospect in the Dodgers' organization behind third baseman Andy LaRoche, who is currently on the Dodgers' main 40-man roster.

"He's done very well down here at spring training," Parrish said of Kershaw. "He's got a fantastic arm and it has been very impressive. We'll just see how it works out."

Mattingly was the 31st overall pick in the 2006 draft. The son of former New York Yankees' great Don Mattingly is one of the top 10 Dodgers prospects according to Baseball America.

"Preston signed last year and did a real good job in the Gulf Coast League," Parrish said. "He hit .290 so they liked what they see in him."

Kershaw heads a pitching staff that is expected to be a pretty formidable one.

"We have some very good arms in this camp,"

Parrish said. "I think the pitching staff that we're putting together right now is going to be pretty effective up there.

Parrish and the Dodgers are very careful about trying to bring players along too fast.

"You don't want to rush people and I think that's one of the big mistakes. They might get into a league where they could be in over their head. They struggle and it creates doubts in their mind of how good they are."

The final Loons roster will be determined by what the other Dodgers' minor league teams do.

"They're (the Dodgers) are still in the process of moving some guys," Parrish said. "A lot of that is dictated by the Major League team. Even though we're only a low 'A' team, when the Major League team makes moves, it has a trickle-down effect for everyone else." ■

LEFT: Dodgertown assistant equipment manager Joe Comando, of Camarillo, Calif., searches for a new bat to replace the broken Louisville Slugger over his shoulder. Comando's daily responsibilities include providing new bats and uniforms along with washing over 250 uniforms from four different minor league teams. "It's almost like there's no way I can do all of this by tomorrow but you just pick at it," Comando said of facing the mountains of dirty laundry on a daily basis.

Photo by Brett Marshall

BELOW: Dodgers minor league catcher Kenley Jansen takes batting practice during spring training.

Photo by Brett Marshall

RIGHT: Clayton Kershaw delivers a pitch during the Dodgers' minor league game against the Cardinals during spring training. Kershaw threw on average over 90 miles per hour. Photo by Brett Marshall

OPPOSITE TOP: Loons hitting coach Garey Ingram jokes with players and head coach Lance Parrish before the Dodgers' minor league team takes the field for a game against the Mets during spring training. Photo by Brett Marshall

OPPOSITE BOTTOM: Great Lakes Loons manager Lance Parrish was a picture of concentration during spring training. Photo by Brett Marshall

Stavropoulos Takes In Spring Training

By Chris Marchand

William Stavropoulos gazed at a mural in the staff lounge at Dodgertown highlighting the 1955 World Series champions.

"I was at the final game," he said. "I still can see Sandy Amoros making that catch."

Stavropoulos, the retired chairman of the board of The Dow Chemical Co. was the driving force to bring the Great Lakes Loons to Midland. He, his wife Linda and a few friends made the three-hour trip Wednesday from their winter home in Naples, Fla., to get a look at Dodgertown.

"Vero Beach is Dodgertown, and it's going to disappear in a year," he said. "I wanted to make sure that I saw it before they left."

The catch Stavropoulos was referring to was Amoros' diving catch on a line drive from the New York Yankees' Yogi Berra in the sixth inning of Game 7 of the World Series at Yankee Stadium. The catch helped the then-Brooklyn

Dodgers win the game and the series.

Stavropoulos, the founder and president of the Michigan Baseball Foundation, which owns the Loons, got a guided tour from Dodgers' assistant director of player development Chris Haydock.

Haydock rattled off little-known facts about Dodgertown. One is that Dodgertown is one of just three spring training complexes that have on-site housing for players.

"You look at why you're affiliated with a team?" Haydock said. "One, it was the history. If you look at the premier franchises in the league, the Dodgers have to be in the top three. Then, the people that are associated with the Dodgers are first-class. We're very fortunate to be associated with them."

"It's going to be electric," Stavropoulos said. "Tommy Lasorda is going to be there. We're going to have a whole group of folks there. It's going to be a lot of fun."

The only question that remains is who will don the Loons' uniforms and what will the weather be like.

"When we announced the team last January, it was a nice day," Stavropoulos said. "I said that I hope it's like this on opening day. Boy, I hope it is." ■

ABOVE: Great Lakes Loons founder and president William Stavropoulos along with his wife, Linda, and friends receive a guided tour from the Dodgers assistant director of player development Chris Haydock Wednesday afternoon.

Photo by Brett Marshall

LEFT: Great Lakes Loons founder and president William Stavropoulos checks out the view from the staff lounge as he, his wife Linda, and friends receive a guided tour with Dodgers assistant director of player development Chris Haydock. Photo by Brett Marshall

BELOW: "He wouldn't know where else to go during spring break," Chad Ashley said of his son Drew, 7, who's been to the Dodgers' spring training every year since his birth. The pair along with Chad's wife, Lucy, and daughter, Claire, 5, watched as one of their favorite players, Preston Mattingly, son of Don Mattingly, took the field. "The Dodgers were the team when I was a kid and it just stuck," Ashley said. Photo by Brett Marshall

ABOVE: Dodgers minor league center fielder Bridger Hunt slides safely into second base beneath a leaping Juan Rivera during a game between the Midland and San Bernardino teams. Photo by Brett Marshall

RIGHT: Dodgers minor league shortstop Justin Fuller makes a catch at second base to get Cardinals' William Sandoval out during a preseason game hosted by the Dodgers. Photo by Brett Marshall

PREVIOUS: Dodgers minor league pitcher Jesus Rodriguez winds up against a Mets minor league batter during their game at the Dodgertown complex. The Dodgers won the game 7-4 with three of those runs coming in the bottom of the ninth inning. Photo by Brett Marshall

OPPOSITE TOP: Dodgers minor league outfielder Scott Van Slyke, right, talks with his older brother A.J., minor league first baseman for the St. Louis Cardinals, before the start of their pre season games at the Dodgertown complex. Photo by Brett Marshall

ABOVE: A panoramic view of the Los Angeles Dodgers' preseason game against the Cleveland Indians from the press box at Holman Stadium in Vero Beach, Fla.

Photo by Brett Marshall

RIGHT: Dodgers' minor league field coordinator P.J. Carey, left, and Dodgers' minor league pitching and hitting coordinator Marty Reed check out the Dodgers' single A minor league game against the Cardinals from their golf carts.
Photo by Brett Marshall

BELOW: Preston Mattingly, left, Scott Van Slyke and Shane Justis await the next fly ball while shagging balls in the outfield during batting practice. *Photo by Brett Marshall*

Two Familiar Names At Camp

By Chris Marchand

It may be a new team with a new stadium and new players. But two potential names on the Great Lakes Loons' opening day roster will be familiar to many baseball fans.

Scott Van Slyke and Preston Mattingly are both following in the footsteps of their famous fathers.

Mattingly's father, Don Mattingly, played for the New York Yankees from 1982-95. He was a six-time All-Star, a nine-time Gold Glove winner at first base, and was the American League Most Valuable Player in 1985.

The younger Mattingly played last season in the Gulf Coast League for the Dodgers. He had a standout high school career at Evansville Central High School in Indiana.

"In high school, my dad never made me play anything," Mattingly said. "He said, if I wanted to play baseball, play baseball; if I wanted to play basketball, play basketball;

if I wanted to play football, play football. I ended up playing all three. He had no influence on anything that I did. He just let me do whatever I wanted to do."

Mattingly, a 6-foot, 3-inch shortstop, was drafted by the Dodgers in the supplemental first round of the 2006 draft. He batted .290 with 29 RBIs in 48 games last season in the Rookie League.

"It was awesome," Mattingly said of being picked by the Dodgers. "I just wanted to get drafted by anybody. It's a kid's dream to get drafted by a Major League team. I didn't care where I went. I just wanted to play."

He originally planned on playing college baseball at Tennessee. But after being drafted so high, he elected to bypass college and head straight to pro ball.

Not surprisingly, Mattingly was introduced to baseball at an early age and got to mingle with some of the game's greats.

"It was great being around the clubhouse when I was young and getting to meet all the great players that my dad played with," he said. "It was a great time for me, but I just want to put that behind me and make my own way with the Dodgers."

So, what does he remember most about growing up with the Yankees?

"They were bad, but I'll try to think of one," Mattingly said. "I think the playoffs in 1995, that was an awesome experience. To go to the playoffs and play the Mariners, that was a good experience for me."

As spring training comes to an end, Mattingly isn't concerned where he plays. He just wants an opportunity.

ABOVE: Dodgers minor league shortstop Preston Mattingly, right, jokes with fellow infielder Shane Justis during batting practice. Photo by Brett Marshall

"I'll play wherever they put me. I just want to play," he said.

He also knows that playing in the majors like his dad isn't going to be easy.

"Everybody here can play," he said. "Everyone works hard and they want to move up. Everyone's goal here is to play in the majors. Everyone working for one thing. It's all one big competition."

Scott Van Slyke is in his second season with the Dodgers' organization. After a standout career at John Burroughs High School in St. Louis, Van Slyke was drafted in the 14th round by the Dodgers in the 2005 draft.

He spent last season at Ogden in the Pioneer League under current Loons' manager Lance Parrish. He batted .256 with 17 RBIs in 45 games.

Van Slyke's father, Andy Van Slyke, played for St. Louis from 1983-86 and Pittsburgh from 1987-94. He helped the Cardinals advance to the World Series in 1985. While in Pittsburgh, he played on some formidable teams that featured the likes of Barry Bonds and Bobby Bonilla. His son got to experience life with the Pirates first-hand.

"It was a lot of fun, especially being able to travel as much as I did," the younger Van Slyke said. "A lot of kids don't get to travel at all. Going to San Francisco and all those places you normally have to wait 20 to 30 years to see (was great). I was very lucky and fortunate to meet the kind of players that I did and see how they acted around the clubhouse." ■

RIGHT: Loons hitting coach Garey Ingram hits fly balls to outfielders during practice.
Photo by Brett Marshall

ABOVE: Loons hitting coach Garey Ingram reacts after outfielder Bridger Hunt sent a ball deep into the outfield during batting practice. Ingram and pitching coach Glenn Dishman watched as the team batted, occasionally commenting on what the players needed to work on. Photo by Brett Marshall

BELOW: Dodgers minor league pitcher David Pfeiffer, of Ft. Pierce Fla., takes a few practice swings before the start of another day of spring training. "It's a little easier than it was last year," Pfeiffer, a fourth year player, said.

Photo by Brett Marshall

RIGHT: Tommy Giles, of Vero Beach, Fla., translates popular English phrases into Spanish with the help of fellow teammate Eduardo Perez, of Venezuela, while in the dugout.

Photo by Brett Marshall

BELOW: Kenley Jansen, of Curacao, left, Eduardo Perez, of Venezuela, Carlos Santana, of the Dominican Republic, and Tommy Giles of Vero Beach, Fla., joke in the dugout as their teammates take their turn at bat during the Dodgers' minor league game against the Cardinals. Jansen, Perez, and Santana took time to help Giles with his Spanish. Giles returned the favor with their English.

Photo by Brett Marshall

OPPOSITE: "This year's spring training has been fantastic," Great Lakes Loons manager Lance Parrish said reflecting on his time in Vero Beach, Fla. Parrish said he has enjoyed the opportunity to be part of the "rich tradition" that the Dodgers have established at Dodgertown. "I'm excited that I've been here this year and excited that we had the weather that we did, but I'm also excited to get out of here and start the season," Parrish said.

Photo by Brett Marshall

CHAPTER SIX

Loons... On and Off the Field

Paul Barbeau, the Man In Charge

By Fred Kelly

They say that time flies when you're having fun.

If so, Paul Barbeau must be having a blast, because time is whizzing by at warp speed.

"It's been a blur, for sure. It's been a quick year," Barbeau said as he approached his one-year anniversary as president and general manager of the Great Lakes Loons.

"It's been stressful at times but not overly stressful. ... It's been a lot of incredible positive energy," he added. "Any stress has been offset by the quality of people we have here."

Barbeau, 34, might shrug off the notion of being stressed out, but there can be no arguing that he has been a very busy man over the past 12 months. Since arriving in Midland a year ago, he has been working at breakneck pace to ensure that the Loons — and Dow Diamond — will be ready for opening day.

"The timeline we're on has been a huge challenge," Barbeau admitted. "We're designing and building a stadium in a year. We're building a franchise in a year."

ABOVE: Paul Barbeau hugs his son Peter, 2, at his office. Photo by Kevin Benedict

LEFT: "It's not your everyday niche, but everybody has to find one," Dow Diamond grounds crew worker Charlie Dijak, of Saginaw, said of his specialty, painting logos on the field. Dijak has been painting on playing fields since his freshman year in high school. "This is living a dream. I've always wanted to do this," Dijak said of the job that promoted him from painting lines on high school football fields. Photo by Brett Marshall

" ... Every part of it, from the stadium to the staff to the ticket sales, was jumping in all at once," he added. "It's been a big, big challenge and one we're still working through."

He said he felt well equipped to handle that challenge after spending 11 seasons, including eight as general manager, for the Class A Spokane Indians. Still, he noted, working for an established organization is a far cry from building a team from scratch — particularly a team that will play twice as many games as Spokane.

"It's completely different (with the Loons) because of the interest level and the excitement," he said.

Another big difference, Barbeau added, is that there's no time to focus on the small stuff when you're getting a team off the ground. There's just too much big stuff to get done first.

He said he used to spend days and even weeks poring over minor stadium improvements, promotions and such when he was in Spokane.

"Now, those details seem so small, while here we need to get the big-picture stuff up and running," he said. "Once we get those going, we can focus on those details."

And those details are important, even if they are on the back burner for now, Barbeau said.

As he pointed out, keeping things fresh for fans after the initial honeymoon period is over is the key to growth.

"If we commit ourselves to being the best franchise in minor league baseball, that's the goal. That's certainly what we strive to do, and I think that's how you maintain or even grow your attendance over time," Barbeau said.

The way to do that, he added, is to continue being active in the community, continually provide new entertainment and promotions, keep the stadium looking good and, perhaps most importantly, keep an enthusiastic, friendly staff at the ballpark and in the office.

"It's like any other business. You know the good customer service places from the not-so-good or average ones," he noted. "Those details are hugely, hugely important. I think that's what separates a good minor league franchise from a great one — that attention to the smallest detail."

That will be a tall task, admitted Barbeau, who came from a situation in Spokane where he was responsible for only 38 home games. By contrast, the Loons will play a 70-game home schedule.

"Talk about family adjustments. That's probably the biggest one," he said with a grin. "That's a personal challenge, certainly, just because those are long work days, and those are nights and evenings

and weekends that you're away from your family."

Barbeau said the challenge of keeping things interesting for the fans through a 70-game home schedule is both daunting and exciting.

"Just keeping yourself up and energized and enthused can be tough when you're in an eight-game homestand in July and it's your 50th-some game," he said. "But I think a lot of times the energy of the ballpark kind of carries you through. ... It's a bit of a challenge, but it's one that's pretty exciting."

Barbeau said his family — wife Shauna and 2-year-old son Peter — has adjusted well to the move to Midland and his long work hours. A lot of that, he said, has to do with the many relationships they've already established.

"We're enjoying it. It's been a great experience," he said. "People are so excited about baseball and have really made an effort to welcome us. We've made a lot of good friends and met lots of people over the past year."

He added that Shauna sometimes misses her parents and brothers, who still live in Spokane. In fact, he first met her when he was working for the Indians.

"Leaving (family behind) can be challenging on some days, and obviously my work year has been pretty busy," he said. "But we knew all of that (when we came to Midland), and we were ready for that.

" ... I owe a lot to Minor League Baseball," he added. "But probably top on that list is meeting my wife and starting my family."

Barbeau, himself, is also far from home. A native of Peabody, MA, a suburb of Boston, he said his parents still live in the same house where he grew up.

He recalled a time when he was about 7 years old, and his mother falsified his age slightly so he could enter a contest in which the prize was admission to a daylong Red Sox clinic.

"I probably shouldn't say that as we're getting ready to start our own promotions," Barbeau said with a laugh, adding that his older sister also entered the contest. "I ended up winning, and my sister did not. She was all upset.

"It was a tough family moment, but she got over it," he added with another laugh.

Barbeau's lifelong passion for the Red Sox runs so deep that, when Shauna was pregnant with Peter back in Spokane, they sometimes had to make tough choices between attending birthing classes or watching the 2004 postseason on TV.

"We skipped a few (classes), to be honest," Barbeau admitting, smiling. "And my wife was very supportive of that. She understood how special this was." ■

Brad Golder ... voice of the Loons

By Dan Chalk

One week after arriving in Midland, Brad Golder is realizing just how exciting an endeavor he has joined.

"I go to the grocery store and I tell people that I'm going to be broadcasting for the Loons, and their eyes get big and they can't believe it," said Golder, who has been hired as the Great Lakes Loons' first radio play-by-play broadcaster and director of broadcasting and media relations.

Like Ernie Harwell many years before him, Golder is a young man from Georgia embarking on a baseball broadcasting career in Michigan.

He will make history as the first voice of the Class A Loons, broadcasting all 140 of the team's games on WYLZ-FM 100.9 (WHEELZ 101). Some games may be televised as well.

Golder, 25, said he understood he was selected from about 170 applicants.

"I really jumped at the opportunity," said Golder, who was the operations manager for the Atlanta Braves' radio broadcasts the past two seasons. "I know there were a lot of candidates for the job, but I think I showed them that I really wanted it, and wanted the opportunity to be a part of a brand-new tradition of baseball here in the Great Lakes area."

Golder will make his debut at the Loons' inaugural game on the evening of Thursday, April 5, when they visit the South Bend (Ind.) Silver Hawks. Before that, he will broadcast updates from the Los Angeles Dodgers' spring training in Vero Beach, Fla. The Loons are a Dodgers' affiliate.

Loons' President and General Manager Paul Barbeau and Loons' Assistant GM - Marketing and Promotions Chris Mundhenk were impressed with Golder when they met him at baseball's winter meetings in Orlando, Fla., early in December. They offered him the job before leaving Orlando.

"We wanted someone that was professional and enjoyable to listen to, and also someone that could handle the media relations portion of the job," Barbeau said. "Brad really fit that whole package and carried himself well, and was a good

ABOVE: "I get paid to watch baseball, there's nothing better I could do," Dow High student Alex Faust, 17, said of his job as a section leader at Dow Diamond. Faust's duties included wiping seats, crowd control, and "most importantly" checking on foul balls and making sure people are okay. Photo by Brett Marshall

ABOVE LEFT: Brad Golder, Great Lakes Loons play-by-play announcer, calls the game against the South Bend Silver Hawks on Wheelz 101 (100.9-FM) and online at loons.com.
Photo by Alex Stawinski

LEFT: Brad Golder, Great Lakes Loons play-by-play announcer, has a great view of the Dow Diamond field from his announcing area.
Photo by Alex Stawinski

fit for us."

Barbeau hopes to see Golder work his way up the ranks to the major leagues.

"We want to help him be the first Loon in the major leagues, and have our fans look back and remember him when he was here," Barbeau said.

Golder said his major influences as a broadcaster are Braves' broadcasters Skip Caray, Pete Van Wieren, Don Sutton and Joe Simpson.

"And I was lucky enough to work with all four the past two seasons. ... Hopefully I've learned something from them along the way," Golder said.

Golder also got to hang out with players he had followed for years as a Braves' fan growing up in Marietta, Ga.

"It's one of those things you kind of dream of your whole life — you're on a team charter plane with John Smoltz and Chipper Jones. It was kind of like living a dream," Golder said.

Golder said his style is to paint a picture of the action for the viewer without being overly dramatic.

"I like to think I'm conversational," he said. "I'm not going to sound like I'm doing a monster truck rally or anything like that. I think any excitement you hear from me is going to be legitimate. A base hit in the third inning is not going to sound like it's in the seventh game of the World Series.

"The way I'll talk to you when I see you at the barber shop is the same way I'll talk to you when I'm on the air," Golder continued. "I've heard that people want to hear a broadcast that sounds like two guys at a sports bar talking, and hopefully it's going to sound like I'm at a sports bar just talking about sports."

Golder also looks up to longtime Dodgers' broadcaster Vin Scully, ESPN's Dan Shulman, and Harwell, the Hall of Fame broadcaster who called Detroit Tigers' game for 42 years.

Golder said that he will broadcast the games by himself, but that some games may also feature a color commentator.

"We are still determining whether we want to hire a color commentator for home games, and there's still a possibility that some games will be televised," Golder said. "Any TV games we do will likely have a color commentator."

During the season, Golder will juggle his duties as a broadcaster and as director of media relations. ■

On the Mic ... Jerry O'Donnell

By Dan Chalk

In 25 years of public speaking, Jerry O'Donnell has never had an assignment quite like this.

O'Donnell's voice will welcome thousands of Great Lakes Loons' fans to 60 home games at the new Dow Diamond, starting April 13. He was recently named the Loons' public address announcer.

"I know those several thousand people in the stands are going to be anticipating being part of the national pastime (of baseball)," said O'Donnell, 42. "I'm humbled and thrilled that they're going to let me be the voice of that pastime here in Midland."

It will be O'Donnell's job to introduce each batter during the game, announce the score between innings and make various other announcements.

O'Donnell and his wife, Carrie, live in Midland with their sons, Jordan, 8, and Jared, 6, who both play baseball.

"I have a sense of awe at the power and magic of the game of baseball," O'Donnell said. "It's as

close to a state religion as we have in America. Baseball is the same wherever you go."

Dennis Hutchinson, news director and mid-day host at radio station WUGN FM-99.7 (Family Life Radio) will be the PA announcer for the 10 Sunday home games.

Dennis Beson of the local band The Sinclairs will be the Loons' on-field host.

O'Donnell is a TV news producer and associate radio producer who also does voice-overs for WNEM TV5/WNEM AM-1250. He recently worked at radio station WGER FM-106.3, and has been a longtime announcer at the Dow Corning Tennis Classic.

ABOVE: Great Lakes Loons announcer Jerry O'Donnell makes pre-game notifications during the final game of the Loons' 2007 inagural season at Dow Diamond Monday, September 3, 2007. Photo by Alex Stawinski

RIGHT: Dow Diamond head grounds crew worker Matt McQuaid cuts the grass near the warning track before a game. Photo by Brett Marshall

"I have been in radio since 1981," he said. "I turned on the microphone on October 31, 1981, at a little station in Frankfort, Michigan. I celebrate my radio birthday on Halloween."

O'Donnell was one of about 100 people who auditioned for the job on Feb. 13 at Saginaw Valley State University, evaluated by a panel of Loons' staff members.

"His enthusiasm and experience, and just his on-mic presence really wowed us," said Loons' Promotions Manager Linda Uliano, who was part of the panel.

"There were a lot of really terrific voices that I heard (at the auditions)," O'Donnell said. "I just thought I'd give it my best shot and put my energy and personality on the microphone and see what happens."

He looks forward to testing the microphone at the stadium.

"I can't wait to try out the mic and see what I sound like at Dow Diamond," he said. I may have to play with the mic to get the right sound out of the instrument."

Growing up in the small town of Bendon, near Interlochen, O'Donnell sang and played the trombone, tuba, baritone and sousaphone. He hinted that he will call upon that musical background when he introduces the Loons' players.

"I'm not going to tell you what I'm going to do to introduce the Loons, but my experience as a tuba player is part and parcel to my introduction of the Loons," he said. "I have physical attributes that will absolutely need to be called upon to do the performance.

"I have a lot of things planned that should be fun and should give Dow Diamond its own signature sound," O'Donnell added. ∎

Lou E. Loon a Hit With Fans

By Dan Chalk

To Laura Ratkos, the best part about the Great Lakes Loons isn't the players, although she likes them a lot.

It's not the postgame fireworks, which are great too.

It isn't even Dow Diamond itself.

For this devoted Loons' fan, the best reason to spend a night at the ballpark is that fluffy ball of feathers, Lou E. Loon, the team mascot.

"He has the most character of any mascot I've seen," said Laura, who is a senior teller at LaSalle Bank, where her co-workers affectionately call her a Lou E. "stalker."

"People would ask me, 'Have you seen Lou E.? What's Lou E. been up to?'" Laura said with a laugh.

"It's a real good talking point with your customers," she added. "It kind of like brings your community together. It's fun to share who's been to the game."

Laura and her family live just two blocks from Dow Diamond and can see the scoreboard from the bay window of their Grove Street home when the leaves are off their trees. She and her husband, Ed, attended 27 Loons' games this season — giving them plenty of chances to meet Lou E.

"I've got his autograph, and I've got lots of pictures of Lou E.," Laura said. "He's just an adorable mascot."

Ed agreed that his wife is into Lou E. big time.

"Sometimes we're close to him when he comes by," Ed said. "He does a high five with her. She enjoys that very much."

Laura said that Lou E. really gives the fans their money's worth.

"He's real approachable as a mascot. He's real visible," she said. "Some (stadiums), you go and you never see the team's mascot. You can see him doing

ABOVE: Lou E. Loon, the official mascot for the Great Lakes Loons, practices for his guest appearance in the Men of Music's baseball-themed show, Play Ball, at the Midland Center for the Arts.

Photo by Jason Johns

some really funny stunts. We always go in and the game starts and we go, 'Where's Lou E. at?'"

Ed, meanwhile, has another reason to enjoy the games.

"I always bring a glove (to the games)," said Ed, who works for Dollar Days. "I got three (foul balls) this year."

The family has been into the Loons since the stadium was being built last year.

"I was watching it being built the whole time," Laura said. "We were there for the first game, even though it was bitterly cold. We got hooked on going. It's just a great environment."

Laura and Ed's younger son, Jordan, 16, also goes to a lot of the games.

"His friends can come and they can walk over (to the stadium) as a group, and we don't have to worry where they're at," Laura said. "The ballpark overall is one of the nicest things that's happened to Midland. It's not expensive. It's a nice wholesome activity. You can take your kids and not worry about language."

Laura said she's become a much bigger baseball fan since the Loons came to town.

"I would watch the Tigers and things (before)," she said. "But with the team coming to town, I really got hooked on baseball like I never did before."

Laura noted that the Loons' players are a great part of the appeal as well.

"It's sad and good at the same time when they move up and leave our team," she said. "You'd like

them to win every game. But it's really nice just to watch the guys grow, because you know you're seeing some future stars.

"The team players make good role models for the smaller children," Laura added.

"I got to see (former Loons' manager) Lance Parrish and shake his hand," Ed said. "I met (outfielder) Bridger Hunt before he got moved up."

The Loons were a rallying point for the Ratkos' neighborhood during the season, Laura said.

"Everybody comes over and meets before the games," she said. "We're always getting with our friends and finding out who's got tickets. If

we have extra tickets, we share tickets. It's a nice neighborhood thing." ∎

ABOVE: Lou E. Loon greets children as they run the bases after the Great Lakes Loons game at Dow Diamond September 2, 2007.
Photo by Alex Stawinski

BELOW: Five-year-old Joshua Kaiser gives Lou E. high ten during a game against the Clinton Lumber Kings. "Caleb always wants to see Lou E.," Kaiser said of his 2-year-old younger brother. The pair visited the mascot on more than one occasion during the game. Photo by Brett Marshall

ABOVE: Ken Johnson, right, of Chemical Bank, holds a briefcase, attached to his wrist via handcuff, containing $2,000 that was later dropped from a helicopter that Johnson boarded at Dow Diamond. The money was scattered across the field and then picked up by contestants. At left is Ben Gurnee, who works for the Great Lakes Loons. Photo by Kevin Benedict

LEFT: Ben Stansbury, 17, of Saginaw, works at the Philly cheesesteak cart at Dow Diamond during a Loons game in July alongside Debbie Beiser, of Auburn, at left. "I think we're by far the most popular thing here," Stansbury said, "other than the beer." Stansbury said that on average they sell about 200 cheesesteaks each game night.

Photo by Kevin Benedict

ABOVE: Catering and kitchen services manager Shantel Lawson jokingly nudges future Dow Diamond dish washer Ned Anderson as she passes while giving her employees a tour of the stadium's kitchen area. The tour was the first time many of the employees had seen the inside of the stadium. Photo by Brett Marshall

RIGHT: On-field host Dennis Beson reacts after getting a plate-full of something in the face during a Loons game on July 31. Photo by Kevin Benedict

ABOVE: Grounds crew members Shelly Fiting, left, and Keith Winter, right, tamp down a mixture on the away team bullpen at Dow Diamond as John Fleeman observes. Photo by Kevin Benedict

LEFT: Lohmann Sports Fields employees Sergio Jordan, left, and Ignacio Zamora work on tightening up the seams of freshly laid sod in the outfield at the Dow Diamond in October 2006.

Photo by Brett Marshall

CHAPTER SEVEN

The Home Opener

Opening Night ... A Great Park
By Chris Stevens

Christine Yax was probably like a lot of area baseball fans Thursday night.

She couldn't sleep.

She was too excited about the Great Lakes Loons playing their home opener in the brand-new Dow Diamond.

To her, and no doubt to many, many others from ages 6 to 86, it was like having Christmas morning on April 13th.

In this case, the present was a $33 million ballpark in downtown Midland, and a Class A minor league team to watch.

"I kept thinking about the 'Field of Dreams' movie. If we build it, they will come," Yax said a couple hours before game time.

Yax was wiping down seats behind the home-plate screen and making them nice and clean for fans, who finally got their chance to enter the stadium shortly after 5 p.m.

As a section leader, Yax got to work before 4 o'clock. She even works a full-time job at Pat's Gradall in Midland.

This is a part-time gig, but one she's excited about. She was so excited, in fact, that it caused a restless night of sleep Thursday night.

Now that's Christmas-like excitement, something that motivates her on the job.

"My job is to make sure it's safe and clean for the fans," she said with a smile.

Not too far from Yax was another new Loons' employee — 80-year-old Ed Tuma, who wore a smile about as big as the bag he was toting as he

ABOVE: Fans watch from a grassy area beyond right centerfield as the Great Lakes Loons take on the Lansing Lugnuts during their first home game in franchise history. Photo by Jason Johns

LEFT: Great Lakes Loons pitcher Cody White holds a ball in his tattered batting glove between hitting ground balls to the infielders during batting practice. Photo by Brett Marshall

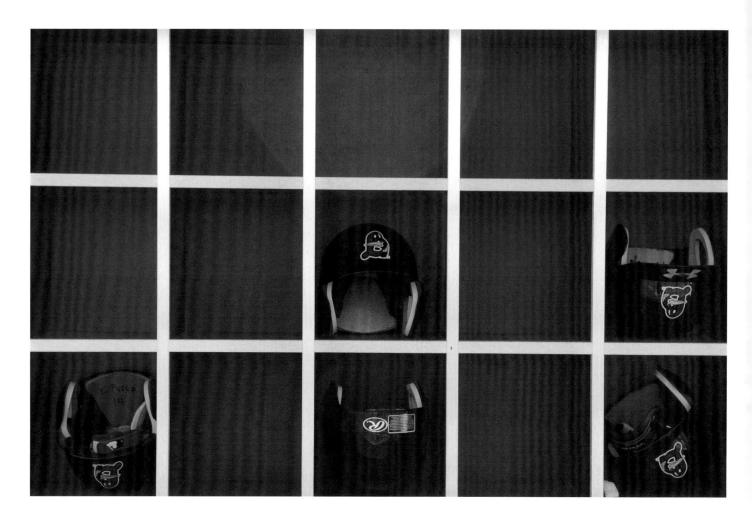

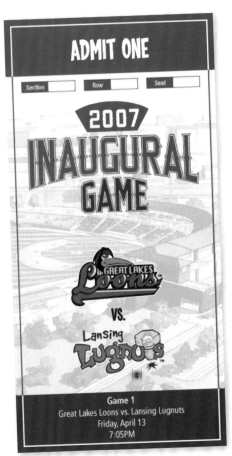

carried game programs.

"I think I'm going to sell out of these," he remarked, even before the gates opened.

Tuma, who many Midlanders might remember as the former owner of Cafe Edward on Bay City Road, was upbeat and positive about the Loons finally taking flight in Midland.

"I think this is going to be a great thing for Midland and the whole area," he said. "The spirit is great. The organization is committed to the fans. I'm looking forward to the season."

He was asked about the stadium.

"It's beautiful," he said. "You can't beat this park. It's something else."

Fred Eddy will love hearing that.

Eddy was the project manager for Dow Diamond, and was given the tall task of getting the stadium finished in time for the home opener.

"We had a great team," he said. "It was a tremendous challenge, and we accomplished that challenge. For us, this was the plan. It's one of the last days of the plan.

"The whole team worked hard. We had some milestones along the way, and we tried to hit everyone of those."

Now that spectators and ball players are actually inside the stadium, and games are being played, Eddy can sit back and savor the moment. That's a pretty special feeling, especially for a hometown boy like Eddy.

"Now I can watch them and see how they use the place and how they feel about it," he said. "I'm going to be wondering around most of the night, just watching people have fun."

Fun, indeed. ■

ABOVE: Batting helmets line the dugout wall before the start of the Great Lakes Loons' first game.   Photo by Brett Marshall

LEFT: A ticket from the first game of the Great Lakes Loons.

Opening Night Goodies

By Tony Lascari

What were fans craving on the Great Lakes Loons' opening weekend at Dow Diamond?

Besides a victory, they wanted a classic. The hot dog.

"Hot dogs, a beer, fries — that's a ball game," said Midland resident Mike Cline.

After checking out the impressive new stadium Friday night, he and Shaine Cline grabbed a couple $3.50 jumbo dogs and piled on the toppings.

They added onions, relish and mustard, which is the only way to honor the all-beef franks from Dearborn Sausage Co., according to Mike.

"That's the way the hot dogs are supposed to be eaten, off the grill with all the fixings," he said.

Shaine said they have been eating healthy since before Valentine's Day, so going to the game was their chance to indulge.

The dogs have a satisfying taste of their own, but the ability to personalize them could be the key to this ballpark favorite. It's your choice, so go for the ketchup, mustard, onion, relish, mayonnaise or even jalapeño peppers.

One tip: Plan ahead while waiting in line to speed up the process at the condiment stand.

Michael and Kathleen Wood, of Midland, opted for footlong bratwursts from the "Sausage Shack" kiosk instead of the classic hot dog. Complete with onions and green peppers, the $5.50 brats didn't let them down.

"They were actually better than most, and the price wasn't too bad considering other places, like Comerica (Park)," Kathleen said.

Their son, Elliot, went a different route, getting the four chicken tenders for $5.50. His assessment: They are great.

Another can't miss option is the steak fries. You won't get too many for $3.50, but the blend of a crisp outside and warmed-to-perfection inside will satisfy. For a little more money, go for the chili and cheese, too.

If you're sticking to a diet, even at the game you'll be rewarded with a selection of healthier options. There's a grilled chicken sandwich, deli turkey sandwich and even a spring mix salad, all ranging in price from $4 to $5.50.

Drink options range from the healthier milk and water to Coca-Cola brand soft drinks, Budweiser beers and even local micro-brews.

And don't worry, if you've already had a meal and just want to snack, you can fall back on the peanuts and Cracker Jacks to get you through. Or, step up the snack by ordering a root beer float, funnel cake or even banana split.

Whatever you do, don't try it all in one night. There are plenty of games left in the season for sampling. ∎

ABOVE: Great Lakes Loons players Preston Mattingly, left, and Scott Van Slyke, sons of former Major League players Don Mattingly and Andy Van Slyke, respectively, face the media during a press conference at Dow Diamond in April 2007. Photo by Kevin Benedict

ABOVE: Great Lakes Loons manager Lance Parrish, shown in the viewfinder of a television camera, participates in a press conference at Dow Diamond in April 2007. Photo by Kevin Benedict

RIGHT: With television cameras aimed through the glass at the Loons' indoor batting cages, Francisco Felix practices pitching after poor weather conditions kept the team inside during media day in April 2007. Photo by Brett Marshall

Opening Night Game

By Chris Marchand

Steven Johnson reared back and fired a fastball over the outside corner for a strike at 7:15 p.m. on Friday. With that, Great Lakes Loons' baseball officially came to Dow Diamond.

However, the festive mood for baseball enthusiasts was short-lived as visiting Lansing built an early five-run lead and made it stand up in a 6-2 victory in Midwest League action.

The Loons dropped to 4-3 on the season while the Lugnuts, an affiliate of the Toronto Blue Jays, climb to 3-1.

"I really wish that we would have played better," Loons manager Lance Parrish said. "It's not an indication of what kind of team we are. We were a little sluggish swinging the bats and we didn't play the way we're capable of defensively."

The loss was about the only thing that could put a damper on the night's festivities. A sellout crowd of 5,454 was treated to warmer temperatures than expected. The game-time temperature was 49 degrees.

Johnson was thrilled to throw the first-ever pitch at Dow Diamond.

"It was pretty cool," Johnson said. "I wanted it to be a strike and I didn't want him to hit it out of the park. I tried to make it a good one and it

ended up being on the corner. The crowd went wild and it was pretty cool."

But things took a turn for the worse a short time after that. Johnson, the losing pitcher, lasted just two innings, giving up five runs on six hits in two innings.

"I felt good today but things just didn't go my way and they didn't go the team's way," Johnson said. "

The second and third innings proved to be the difference in the game. Loons' starter Steven Johnson, after retiring the side in order in the first, yielded five runs.

Lansing put the first run on the board in the second inning when Travis Snider singled and scored on Josh Bell's double to the wall in center.

The Lugnuts' lead grew to 3-0 later in the inning when Chris Gutierrez looped a single to short right that drove in a pair of runs.

Johnson, who threw a ton of pitches in the second, found himself in trouble again in the third. He gave up back-to-back singles to start the inning. An error by third baseman Josh Bell loaded the bases with no outs.

At that point, Johnson was relieved by Francisco Felix. Shoffit greeted Felix with an

RBI groundout to third to make it 4-0. Yuber Rodriguez's sacrifice fly to center drove home the Lugnuts' fifth run.

"They were fouling of a lot of pitches," Johnson said. "I kept getting ahead of the hitters and I couldn't finish. I guess after throwing a lot of pitches, my control wasn't there anymore. It wasn't what I wanted but it happens."

Meanwhile, the Loons couldn't solve Lansing starter A.J. Wideman. He kept Great Lakes hitless until Bridger Hunt, the ninth batter in the order, ripped a double to left. The Loons managed just four hits off four different Lansing pitchers.

As it has been all season, the Loons' bullpen continued to shine. Felix, Miguel Sanfler and Garrett White combined to give up one run on four hits in seven innings.

"The bullpen has don a great job for us all year," Parrish said. "I don't know how to put a finger on it other than we have some talented

ABOVE: Great Lakes Loons centerfielder Trayvon Robinson prepares to throw the ball in from deep in centerfield during the team's first home game of the season. Photo by Kevin Benedict

Stadium Firsts

First pitches: Former Los Angeles Dodgers' manager Tommy Lasorda, Dow Chemical Co. Chief Executive Officer Andrew Liveris, Michigan Baseball Foundation president and retired Dow CEO William Stavropoulos, appeals court judge Bill Schuette, representing the Gerstacker Foundation, Stephanie Burns, Dow Corning Corp. CEO, Mike Whiting, representing the Herbert H. and Grace A. Dow Foundation, and Bobbie Arnold, representing the Strosacker Foundation.

First hit: Lansing outfielder Travis Snider

First out: Lansing's Chris Gutierrez

First strikeout: Loons' starter Steven Johnson

First RBI: Lansing's Josh Bell

First pickoff: Johnson picks off Bell at second base

First stolen base: Sean Shoffit

First wild pitch: Johnson

First double: John Bell, Lansing

First triple: Travis Snider, Lansing

Loons' first at Dow Diamond

Hit: Bridger Hunt

Run: Trayvon Robinson

RBI: Josh Bell

kids that have the ability to throw the ball."

The Loons finally gave the large crowd something to cheer about in the sixth inning. Three straight singles loaded the bases with one out. Bell reached on an error by the shortstop which drove in Trayvon Robinson to make it 5-1. Matt Berezay drove in the second run with a sacrifice fly.

The rally was halted when reliever Edward Rodriguez got Eduardo Perez to fly to center with the bases loaded. ■

BELOW: Taking a break from their afternoon run, members of the Central Middle School girls track team line the outfield tunnel to get a glimpse of pregame practice before the Loons' home opener against the Lugnuts on April 13, 2007. This is a pretty awesome practice isn't it," eighth-grader Gaia Klotz, 14, said of stopping by the stadium during track practice. Photo by Brett Marshall

ABOVE: "I'm lovin' it so far," Kristina LeFevre, 17, said after watching the opening day ribbon cutting outside of the main gate at Dow Diamond from the upstairs window of the Loon Loft. The gates were opened to the public following the cutting and fans climbed the front stairs for the first home game. Photo by Brett Marshall

BELOW: Former Dodgers manager Tommy Lasorda gives Loons shortstop Preston Mattingly some tips on his swing during batting practice before the first game of the season, April 13, 2007. Photo by Brett Marshall

ABOVE: Great Lakes Loons players Josh Bell, left, and Matt Berezay take batting practice indoors at Dow Diamond in April 2007.
Photo by Kevin Benedict

LEFT: Loons outfielder Trayvon Robinson checks out the construction still under way at Dow Diamond as he and fellow teammates dodge ladders on their way from the indoor batting cages to the team clubhouse. Photo by Brett Marshall

RIGHT: Scott Van Slyke gets ready for an at-bat during the first home game in Great Lakes Loons history at Dow Diamond. Photo by Kevin Benedict

ABOVE: Great Lakes Loons pitcher Doug Brooks, left, high-fives outfielder Trayvon Robinson in the team's dugout before the start of the team's first game. The Loons played before a sold out crowd for their first home game in franchise history. Photo by Brett Marshall

LEFT: Conner Zaia, left, and Andrew Wells, both 9, cheer on the Great Lakes Loons from behind the left field fence during the Loons' first home game in franchise history. Photo by Jason Johns

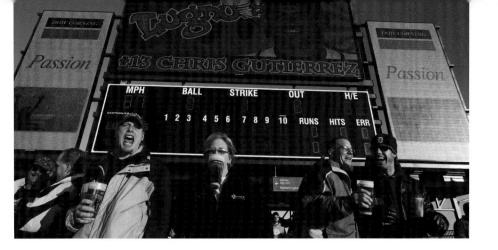

LEFT: Kyle Martek, left, Sandi Christilaw, Corey Seifferly, and Girard Wolf react to the first pitch — a strike thrown at 87 mph — that kicked off the Great Lakes Loons' first home game at Dow Diamond. Photo by Jason Johns

ABOVE: Gaia Klotz, 14, left, Samantha Miller, 14, and Savannah Ludwig, 13, stop for some fun in front of Daddy O's restaurant with the rest of the Central Middle School track team Friday afternoon. The downtown area was filled with tailgate parties for the Great Lakes Loons' first home game in franchise history. Photo by Jason Johns

LEFT: Andrew Wells, 9, left, Conner Zaia, 9, Matthew Brennan, 10, and Jared Lane, 9, react to a play in the 8th inning from their spot in the grass behind the left field wall at the Great Lakes Loons' first home game. "It's awesome, but I can't feel my toes," Brennan said about the game.

Photo by Jason Johns

CHAPTER EIGHT

The Season

Loons Win First Game, Beat South Bend

By Dan Chalk

Lance Parrish had two big reasons to smile late Thursday night.

His Great Lakes Loons had just won the first game of their very first season.

And now they were finally able to get warm.

The Midland-based Loons started their inaugural season with a 10-3 Midwest League victory over the South Bend Silver Hawks at Coveleski Stadium, with a game-time temperature of 32 degrees and icy winds.

"I tell you what, it was pretty cold out there. I'm just happy we're back inside," Parrish said with a grin as he talked to several reporters in the visitors' clubhouse.

Parrish said it was great to win the first game in franchise history.

"It feels very good, very good. It was kind of an endurance test for everybody tonight," he said. "It's always nice to get off to a good start, no matter what the situation, because it creates a little momentum."

Although the official paid attendance was 989, the number of fans in the stands looked to be around 100, and many of them sat in the front couple of rows. A number of other fans, including some from Midland, watched from the suites.

Starter Clayton Kershaw, the top pitching prospect of the Loons' parent club, the Los Angeles Dodgers, struggled with his control and lasted just 2 1/3 innings, giving up two runs, one earned, on two hits and six walks with two strikeouts. He threw 78 pitches.

ABOVE: Loons infielder Justin Fuller bunts in the top of the third inning against the Silver Hawks in South Bend, Ind. Fuller had a walk, scored a run and helped turn two double plays in the game.
Photo by Jason Johns

LEFT: Loons starting pitcher Clayton Kershaw winds up in the second inning against the Silver Hawks in South Bend, Ind. Kershaw was taken out of the game after throwing 78 pitches in 2 1/3 innings. Photo by Jason Johns

"I wanted to see Clayton stick around a little bit longer, but these guys the first month or so are on a pretty strict pitch count, so we had to get him out of there," Parrish said. "But that's all right. At least he got the first (start) under his belt, and he can go from there."

Doug Brooks (1-0) earned the win, taking over for Kershaw and throwing 3 2/3 shutout innings without allowing a hit. ■

VISITOR LINEUP		
21	Robinson	CF
44	Herrera	2B
31	Mattingly	SS
11	Berezay	LF
14	Perez	1B
43	Sutherland	DH
7	Van Slyke	RF
50	Jansen	C
30	Fuller	3B
38	Francisco	P.

ABOVE: The lineup of the Great Lakes Loons is displayed on the concourse level of John O'Donnell Stadium prior to a May 1 game against Swing of the Quad Cities in Davenport, Iowa.
Photo by Kevin Benedict

ABOVE RIGHT: Loons starting second baseman Justin Fuller shouts encouragement to first baseman David Sutherland after an error in the bottom of the second led to the Silver Hawks' first run of the game. The Loons had three errors on the night. Photo by Jason Johns

RIGHT: Eduardo Perez, from Venezuela, huddles in the Loons' dugout trying to keep warm before the season opener against the Silver Hawks in South Bend, Ind. Many players wore face masks in both the warmup and the game.
Photo by Jason Johns

ABOVE: Loons first baseman Eduardo Perez pulls in a throw from Adolfo Gonzalez to force out the Beloit Snappers' runner in the sixth inning. The Loons finished their four game home stand with a 4-0 win. Photo by Jason Johns

BELOW: Great Lakes Loons pitchers Miguel Ramirez, left, Miguel Sanfler and Joe Jones watch a foul ball sail over the fence from their seat in the bullpen Thursday during their game against the Wisconsin Timber Rattlers on Breast Cancer Awareness Night at Dow Diamond. Photo by Jason Johns

PREVIOUS PAGE: The sky is filled with color as the sun sets during this game in May.
Photo by Kevin Benedict

RIGHT: Great Lakes Loons catcher Kenley Jansen runs toward first base in the fifth inning past a breast cancer awareness ribbon painted in the grass at Dow Diamond. The Loons wore pink jerseys in their loss to the Wisconsin Timber Rattlers. Photo by Jason Johns

BELOW: Great Lakes Loons players Bridger Hunt, left, and Trayvon Robinson share a laugh in the dugout before a game against the Wisconsin Timber Rattlers on Breast Cancer Awareness Night at Dow Diamond. The Loons' pink jerseys were later auctioned to fans to raise money for the Pardee Cancer Center at the MidMichigan Medical Center in Midland. "Never in my life did I think I'd wear a pink shirt," Robinson said
Photo by Jason Johns

LOONS RAISE MONEY FOR CANCER

Playing in front of a crowd of 3,822, the Loons wore pink jerseys and auctioned them off during and after the game, raising more than $11,000 to benefit the Pardee Cancer Center at MidMichigan Medical Center in Midland.

Parrish's jersey got the highest bid, selling for $1,550. Loons' pitcher Clayton Kershaw's jersey went for $1,100.

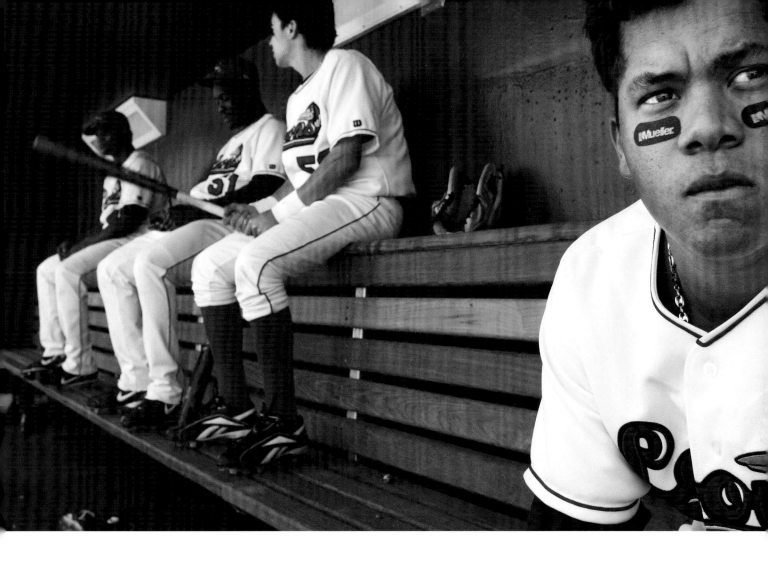

Loons Fall To Lugnuts In Dow Diamond Opener

By Dan Chalk

He was the star of the show. The cheers rang through the chilly night air as Lance Parrish's name was announced and he jogged through the crowd and onto the field for the Great Lakes Loons' very first game at the new Dow Diamond.

"That's the first time I've ever done anything like that," said the Loons' manager and former Detroit Tiger after Friday's home-opening 6-2 loss to the Lansing Lugnuts. "The fans were into it. I think the guys enjoyed it. It was fun."

After the stadium-opening ceremonies, the Lugnuts were introduced and came onto the field and then — in a unique twist — as the Loons were announced, instead of coming onto the field from the dugout, they ran onto the field through an aisle in the stands as their names were called.

Fans high-fived the players as they ran down the aisle.

Parrish was the last one introduced, and he drew the biggest cheers by far.

"It was everything I thought it would be," Par-rish said of the atmosphere at the home opener. "A beautiful ballpark, the best day we've had since we've been here weather-wise, and the crowd was everything that I expected."

It was an opportunity that doesn't come along very often, Parrish noted.

"Once in a great amount of time do you open up a new franchise and a new facility, and — shoot — I had fun," he said with a smile. "I hope everybody that was here had fun, and I hope they'll come back. We're going to have a good club."

Lugnuts' manager Gary Cathcart was on the home team side of a stadium-opening game just two years ago, and he was impressed with Friday's festivities.

"(It was) very well done — great atmosphere, great sight lines, everything was really nice," he said. "(It was) a big day for them. I thought under the circumstances, everything went pretty well for them. I've been involved in a couple of stadium openings over the years, and it's not an easy thing to do." ■

ABOVE: Adolfo Gonzalez sits in the dugout with his teammates, from right, Francisco Lizarraga, Miguel Sanfler and Miguel Ramirez before the start of a game against the Lansing Lugnuts at Dow Diamond. Photo by Tyler Bissmeyer

RIGHT: Miguel Sanfler pitched for the second half of this game against the Lansing Lugnuts.

Photo by Tyler Bissmeyer

BELOW: First baseman Eduardo Perez makes the tag early in the game against a Lansing Lugnut runner at Dow Diamond Stadium. Photo by Tyler Bissmeyer

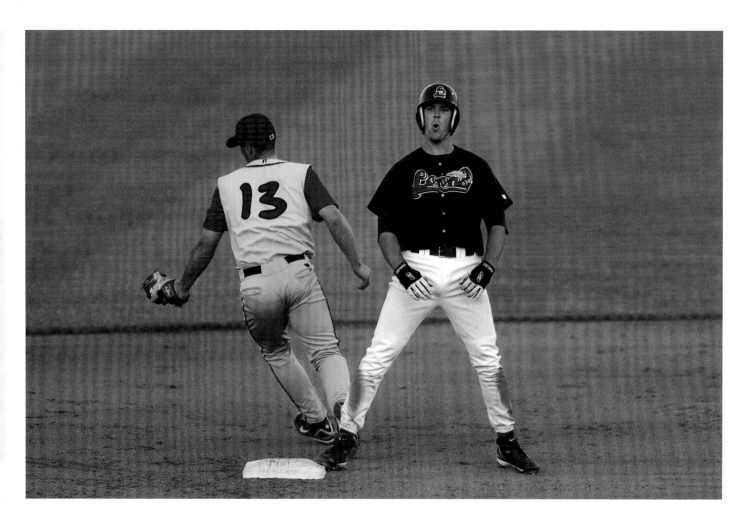

Players Feel Fans' Buzz

By Fred Kelly

Great Lakes Loons' leftfielder Bridger Hunt knows that local baseball fans are crazy about his team.

But even he was thrown a little off-guard by some of the sentiments he heard from Friday's home-opening crowd.

"I heard some guy say he loved me, so I was like, 'OK,'" Hunt said with a chuckle following the Loons' 6-2 loss to Lansing. "That was a first — a guy saying he loved me."

Unexpected declarations of affection aside, Hunt said he thoroughly enjoyed being a part of the Loons' first-ever home game at Dow Diamond.

"It was exhilarating. The fans were great," said the 21-year-old from Lake Mary, Fla. "I sat out in leftfield all night hearing them, and it was just fantastic to have all those people backing you up."

Hunt has the distinction of being the first Loons' player to get a hit at Dow Diamond. His two-out double to leftfield in the bottom of the third inning gave Great Lakes its first baserunner of the evening.

The significance of Friday's game was not lost on Hunt.

"Like Coach (Lance) Parrish said, it's not every day that you get to be on a team where it's a fresh franchise right out of the gates and opening up a new ballpark," Hunt noted. "That's fun, and the (pregame) ceremonies and everything were fun. It was a good time, a great atmosphere today."

Centerfielder Trayvon Robinson, who scored the Loons' first-ever run at Dow Diamond, was all smiles afterward despite the loss.

"I've never played in a stadium like this," Robinson said in a quiet voice with a huge grin on his face. "I went from the Gulf Coast League and no fans (last year) to 5,400 (fans here). I just feel like I'm in the big leagues already."

Robinson said he definitely felt the buzz in the stadium as game time neared.

"Oh, man, the energy was there," he said. "I don't know how to explain it. We were real hyped for the game (to start)."

So hyped, in fact, that waiting for the multi-tude of pregame ceremonies to end proved a bit difficult for Robinson.

"I was just trying to stay stretched out before the game while all of that was going on," said Robinson, a 19-year-old from Los Angeles. "Yeah, I'm glad that's over. We're just going to play ball now." ■

ABOVE: Great Lakes Loons second baseman Preston Mattingly reacts after being called out at second base after a tag from Lansing's Scott Campbell. Photo by Brett Marshall

Loons Pick Up First Home Win

By Chris Marchand

Mired in an eight-game losing streak, the Great Lakes Loons took to the field Saturday night donning their black batting practice jerseys.

The change seemed to work.

A five-run third inning powered the Loons to a historic 5-4 victory over the Cedar Rapids Kernels in a Midwest League battle at Dow Diamond.

"We had been talking about when were going to do it," Loons' manager Lance Parrish said of wearing the black jerseys. "I originally said to wait until Sunday. But we figured we might as well start today and try and change things around. It worked."

The win was the first for the Loons at Dow Diamond. It also ended the Loons' eight-game losing streak and raised their record to 5-10. Cedar Rapids, an affiliate of the Los Angeles Angels of Anaheim, falls to 7-5 on the season.

Trayvon Robinson collected two hits to lead the Loons' offense.

The win was a relief to not only Parrish, but his players as well.

"It was fun," Loons' outfielder Scott Van Slyke said. "Everyone looked like they were pretty excited when they came out of the dugout. It's nice to get that out of the way so we can start rolling. I know everyone was kind of anxious and feeling a little pressure to get that first win after losing the first few (at home)."

The Kernels built a 3-0 lead in the third inning. After a Josh Davies single and a walk to Peter Bourjos, Chris Pettit ripped a Thomas Melgarejo pitch over the left field fence for a three-run homer.

The Loons broke out of their slump in the third inning. Two infield singles and a walk loaded the bases with one out. Matt Berezay followed by ripping a 3-2 pitch to right field to drive in a pair of runs to trim the deficit to one. Eduardo Perez then followed with a towering 375-foot opposite-field home run to left center.

The three-run shot gave the Loons a 5-3 lead and sent the sellout crowd of 5,382 to its feet. It was the first lead the Loons have enjoyed at Dow Diamond this season. ■

ABOVE: Great Lakes Loons shortstop Juan Rivera runs down Lansing's Scott Campbell in a pickle. The Loons defeated the Lugnuts 7-3. Photo by Brett Marshall

Kershaw Promoted

By John Kennett

Monday was a bittersweet day for Great Lakes Loons' manager Lance Parrish. The Loons won for only the fifth time in the last 22 games, but Parrish found out that he would be losing two of his players.

Ace pitcher Clayton Kershaw was promoted Monday to the Jacksonville Suns, the Los Angeles Dodgers' Double-A affiliate, while utility player Parker Brooks announced his retirement from baseball to attend law school at Georgetown University.

Even though the two roommates are headed in different directions, Parrish feels that both will be successful.

"The irony is that they can both end up being extremely successful in different fields," said Parrish. "I have a feeling that Parker is going to be somebody special, and obviously I feel the same way about Clayton.

"Time will tell, but I feel that both of them are going to do pretty well in life," added Parrish.

Parrish realizes that Kershaw, who the Dodgers have on the fast track to the major leagues, is ready for the new challenges that Double-A ball will bring.

"Obviously, (the Dodgers') goal was to get him out of here and give him a taste of Double-A before the season was over," said Parrish. "I think he is ready for that. (Is he) completely ready? I don't know. He still needs to get better command of his pitches.

"He certainly has the stuff. Maybe moving up to a team in first place and being able to pitch against Double-A hitters will help him focus a little better," added Parrish.

Loons' pitching coach Glenn Dishman agreed.

"At this level, he knew that he could sit there and throw fastballs by people, and (he) sometimes didn't have command of his fastball the way he needed to," said Dishman. "(At Jacksonville), he will rise to the challenge and know that he needs to hit his spots and still throw a 96 mile-per-hour fastball when he needs to." ∎

RIGHT: Great Lakes Loons pitcher Clayton Kershaw delivers a pitch to Lansing Lugnuts' Scott Campbell during a game in June. The Lugnuts remained scoreless during Kershaw's time on the mound. Photo by Brett Marshall

Loons Light Up Dragons on Fourth of July

The Great Lakes Loons made their first Fourth of July game a memorable one Wednesday, hitting three home runs and shutting out the host Dayton Dragons 5-0 in Midwest League play.

The Loons were coming off an 18-2 loss to Dayton on Tuesday.

Tommy Giles hit a solo homer in the first inning off veteran major league reliever Mike Stanton, who was making a rehabilitation start for the Dragons.

In the second, Juan Apodaca followed singles by James Peterson and Preston Mattingly with a three-run homer, his fifth, to make it 4-0.

Giles went the distance again in the eighth with his third home run of the season and became the first Loons' player to hit more than one homer in a game.

Clayton Kershaw started for the Loons and allowed two hits in four innings. Due to a 50-pitch limit because of Kershaw's upcoming appearance in Sunday's Major League Baseball Futures Game, he was replaced by Thomas Melgarejo (3-5), who threw three innings for the win. Miguel Ramirez pitched the final two innings.

The Dragons left 15 runners on base. ∎

ABOVE: Catcher Carlos Santana watches as Dayton Dragon's players crowd around a player who was hit in the leg with a pitch. Photo by Tyler Bissmeyer

BELOW: Second baseman Preston Mattingly goes for the grounder as a Dayton Dragon runs to second base. Photo by Tyler Bissmeyer

Loons a Smash at Box Office

By Fred Kelly

The Great Lakes Loons may not have always competed well on the field, but they certainly held their own at the box office.

In their inaugural season, the Loons finished fifth in the Midwest League in total attendance, drawing 324,564 fans to Dow Diamond for an average of 4,773 per home game.

That's a far cry from the team's original projections, which, according to General Manager Paul Barbeau, were 220,000 total and 3,000 per game.

After the season got under way and tickets were going fast, the Loons upped their season projections somewhat but never expected the kind of support they received, Barbeau noted.

"As the momentum started building, we thought maybe we could do 270 or 280 (thousand). ... Then, we started thinking maybe we could hit 300 (thousand), but we kind of crashed right through that," Barbeau said." ... We're

thrilled. That's a big number."

The Loons' final numbers are even more impressive considering that they play in a much smaller ballpark than any of the four teams which finished ahead of them in attendance. They also play in a smaller market than all but one of those teams.

The Dayton Dragons, based in Dayton, Ohio, finished first in the Midwest League, averaging over 8,600 fans per game for a season total of 585,348. The Dragons' Fifth Third Field has a capacity of 7,230, and the team has sold out all home games for seven consecutive seasons.

Dayton is the first and only Minor League Baseball team to sell out every home game before the season has even begun.

"They do a fantastic job (of marketing their team)," Barbeau said of the Dragons." ... They do some pretty amazing things. Those are the kinds of results we strive for."

Kane County, West Michigan and Lansing finished second, third, and fourth, respectively, in attendance this year. The capacity of their stadiums ranges from 7,400 to 11,000, and only Kane County, based in Geneva, Ill., has a smaller population base (19,500) than the Loons. ■

ABOVE: Fred Walker of Midland chats with Great Lakes Loons manager Lance Parrish during the game at Dow Diamond in August. Walker was the first person to purchase a full season ticket package at the stadium. "It's been great. I've been to every game. Some people ask me what their record is. I say, 'What does it matter? They played and we cheered'," Walker said.

Photo by Alex Stawinski

All Star Game Coming to Dow Diamond

By Greg Chalfin

The events keep getting bigger at Dow Diamond. Great Lakes Loons' President and General Manager Paul Barbeau announced Friday during the middle of the second inning of the Loons' game that the Midwest League has selected Dow Diamond as the site for the Midwest League's 2008 All-Star game.

"It's a big thing for us, but it's bigger thing for the community," Barbeau said.

Barbeau said the organization found out the news last December but decided to wait until the weeks before this year's All-Star game — which will be played June 19 in Geneva, Ill. — to tell Friday night's sellout crowd at Dow Diamond.

"We had so much going on," Barbeau said. "We hadn't finished the stadium yet. We didn't have a fan base yet. We just said, 'We're going to put this on the back burner.'"

Full- and half-season ticket holders will have an opportunity to purchase All-Star tickets at the end of this season. Fans with partial plans — eight, 16 or 24 game packages — and the general public will have the opportunity to get tickets through a lottery system, Barbeau said.

"Our stadium is of a size and our fan base is of a size where we're going to have more demand than supply on All-Star game weekend," Barbeau said. "We want to find ways to include all of our fans, even if you didn't get a ticket to the game."

Ways that may occur include "fan fest-type activities" outside the ballpark, a home run derby and a skills competition. Barbeau said prices for tickets to the game will not stray far from the prices for regular season Loons' games.

"This event needs to fit in with our overall brand, which is affordable family entertainment," Barbeau said.

The Loons were slotted to host the game about 10 years from now but used the Midwest League's rules to their advantage by petitioning the league to vote on having the All-Star game at Dow Diamond sooner.

"When we bought the franchise, we looked at the list and thought, 'Oh, gosh. Our chance is way down here,'" Barbeau said.

Midwest League executives voted unanimously to have Great Lakes host next year, pushing the Clinton Lumberkings down a slot.

"Bottom line — this is an event that we can expect, at the best, maybe once every 14 years," Barbeau said. ■

TOP: Two Loons players come together attempting to catch a fly ball.   Photo by Kevin Benedict

ABOVE: Great Lakes Loons center fielder Scott Van Slyke catches a fly ball a game in July.

Photo by Brett Marshall

Loons End With a Loss; Team Sells Out 30 Games

By Dan Chalk

Lance Parrish had two strong feelings Monday night: Gratitude for the Great Lakes Loons' fans support all season, and disappointment that his team didn't give the fans a better showing.

The Loons' manager thanked the final Dow Diamond crowd of the Loons' inaugural season — and the 30th sellout — after his team's 6-2 loss Monday night to the Fort Wayne Wizards. Afterwards, the players stood at the stadium exits to thank fans for their support.

"I think the fans have been incredible all summer long," Parrish said. "Through thick and thin, they've supported us, they've cheered us. I haven't heard too many boos or jeers, even though we deserved a lot more (boos) than we got on occasion, believe me — myself included."

The finale's attendance of 5,515 fans put the season mark for Dow Diamond at 324,564, which was fifth out of 14 teams in the Midwest League. The Loons averaged 4,773 fans on their 68 home dates.

Parrish wished his team had rewarded the fans with more wins.

"I was disappointed the way that we played (this season), just flat out. I thought we had a better team than what we showed," he said.

Parrish said it was special to be a part of the Loons' first season.

"We took our share of lumps this summer," he said. "But through it all, we all had a good time, and we were part of the inaugural season here, and we feel pretty fortunate to be in this environment."

Parrish said he doesn't know where he will end up in 2008, but his ultimate goal is to move back up to the major leagues. He was a coach with the Detroit Tigers under then-manager Alan Trammell a few years ago.

"Absolutely, I would come back here (if the Los Angeles Dodgers asked me to)," Parrish said. "But I'm looking to move up just like anybody else. My objective is to get back to the major leagues. If I have to come back here, then I'd be happy to."

For his part, Loons' centerfielder Trayvon Robinson said it would be hard to leave when the players bus out this morning.

"We've had so much support from this town and these fans, it's incredible," said Robinson, who posed for photos with numerous fans at the top of the rightfield stadium entrance. "It's like New York. It's like a mini-New York. I really enjoyed it. I'm going to miss it a lot."

Robinson — one of about a dozen players who were with the Loons the whole season — said the inaugural season has been a thrill for him.

"When I got here, it was a blessing, man. It's incredible that his little town can give so much support to a baseball team through ups and downs," he said.

Robinson is headed home to Los Angeles for a couple of days, then will start at an instructional league in Arizona.

The Loons finished the second half of the Midwest League season at 23-46, and were 57-82 overall.

Monday's game was the 24th Loons' home game that Larry Overton of Midland has attended this season.

"You can relax, forget whatever's going on. You can forget your troubles (when you come to the ballpark)," Overton said.

Overton believes the Loons will continue to draw big crowds for many years.

"Keep (the stadium) secure, keep the price right, make it a good product," he said. "You do those things, and you'll have a sold-out crowd every time."

* Steve Nichols of Saginaw, who retired last November after 30 years at Delphi, spent the Loons' first season as a door guard.

"I was inside all summer (at my previous job)," Nichols said. "This was kind of like a fun job for me."

The highlight of the season for Nichols was being able to brighten one young boy's day.

"I had Lance (Parrish) sign a ball, and I was going to take it home for my daughter," he said. "But there was a 9-year-old kid who hadn't been able to get an autograph. I gave him the ball, and his eyes just lit up." ∎

MIDWEST LEAGUE ATTENDANCE FOR 2007

1. Dayton Dragons (Fifth Third Field, capacity 7,230; Dayton, Ohio) — 585,348 total, 8,608 per game

2. Kane County Cougars (Philip B. Elfstrom Stadium, capacity 7,400; Geneva, Ill.) — 468,869 total, 7,213 per game

3. West Michigan Whitecaps (Fifth Third Ballpark, capacity 10,051; Comstock Park, Mich.) — 377,412 total, 5,469 per game

4. Lansing Lugnuts (Oldsmobile Park, capacity 11,000; Lansing, Mich.) — 341,746 total, 5,177 per game

5. Great Lakes Loons (Dow Diamond, capacity 5,200; Midland, Mich.) — 324,564 total, 4,773 per game

6. Peoria Chiefs (O'Brien Field, capacity 7,500; Peoria, Ill.) — 259,784 total, 3,820 per game

7. Fort Wayne Wizards (Memorial Stadium, capacity 6,516; Fort Wayne, Ind.) — 237,966 total, 3,605 per game

8. Wisconsin Timber Rattlers (Fox Cities Stadium, capacity 5,500; Appleton, Wis.) — 197,511 total, 3,237 per game

9. Cedar Rapids Kernels (Veterans Memorial Stadium, capacity 5,300; Cedar Rapids, Iowa) — 173,219 total, 2,706 per game

10. South Bend Silver Hawks (Stanley Coveleski Regional Stadium, capacity 5,000; South Bend, Ind.) — 149,281 total, 2,332 per game

11. Swing of the Quad Cities (John O'Donnell Stadium, capacity 4,024; Davenport, Iowa) — 148,773 total, 2,254 per game

12. Clinton Lumberkings (Alliant Energy Field, capacity 4,500; Clinton, Iowa) — 114,898 total, 1,714 per game

13. Beloit Snappers (Pohlman Field, capacity 3,501; Beloit, Wis.) — 82,819 total, 1,254 per game

14. Burlington Bees (Community Field, capacity 3,200; Burlington, Iowa) — 66,857 total, 997 per game

Stavropoulos Says First Season a Success

By Dan Chalk

Bill Stavropoulos hopes that the Great Lakes Loons have benefited a lot of people in this region. The founder and president of the Michigan Baseball Foundation knows they've helped him.

"My wife, Linda, never was much into baseball," Stavropoulos said Monday night during the Loons' season finale at Dow Diamond. "Now that's changed. Now she's saying, 'What are we going to do tomorrow for a date when the season is over?'"

Stavropoulos, the former Dow Chemical Co. chairman and CEO, helped launch the idea for a minor league team in Midland about two years ago. Now, he's seeing the fruits of that endeavor.

The season attendance at Dow Diamond was 324,564, which was fifth out of 14 teams in the Midwest League. The Loons averaged 4,773 fans on their 68 home dates.

"It's very gratifying," Stavropoulos said. "We met our expectations and exceeded them in a lot of areas. As far as attendance, we exceeded them almost by 50 percent. We were gunning for 3,000 per game."

Stavropoulos is also pleased with the team's regional fan base.

"Our goal was to make this a regional team, and I think it's turning into that," he said. "The whole region's benefiting from the Loons. If you looked at the attendance here any given night, you'd see a lot of people from Saginaw, Bay City, Clare, the Thumb. We even get some folks from Flint and Mount Pleasant. And we hope to expand our reach even more next year."

Stavropoulos said he's not disappointed in anything, but he's always striving to make things better.

"I don't think anything disappointed us," he said. "I think as we look around and look at our plans and look at our stadium, (there are) just things that you always could do better. And if you stop doing better, that's when you start losing."

Stavropoulos said that Loons' manager Lance Parrish, a former Detroit Tigers' player, was a big

part of the team's popularity with the fans.

"Lance, his personality, how he relates to the fans, to the players, it's all been very, very good," Stavropoulos said. "And of course, he's a Michigan hero. I think he really enjoyed this year, too."

Stavropoulos also praised the fans as well as the national anthem singers and others who performed at Dow Diamond this year.

"The fans have been absolutely spectacular," he said. "They know what this is all about. The fans are probably the best thing that's happened to us.

"The amount of talent that exists in the Tri-City area is just incredible."

Now that the season is over, it's time for the non-profit MBF — which owns and operates the Loons — to take stock of its finances and make decisions about how to give back to the region, Stavropoulos said.

"Part of our charter is to help develop other businesses," he said. "Another part of our charter is to pour back the profits into the community, once we take care of our internal expenses.

"We hope to support youth activities in the Tri-City area over the coming year. It would probably be in the form of grants to do certain things, whether it's a new field or (something else). We're open to suggestions. We want to be an active part of the community."

As for next season?

"I can't wait," Stavropoulos said. ■

ABOVE: Great Lakes Loons center fielder Trayvon Robinson slams into the wall while trying unsuccessfully to catch a ball hit by Joe Dickerson of the Burlington Bees during a game at Dow Diamond. Photo by Kevin Benedict

TOP LEFT: Scott Van Slyke, third from left, waits to board the bus with teammates, from left, Francisco Felix, Kenley Jansen, David Sutherland, Josh Wall, and Steven Johnson shortly after 7 a.m. in April for an eight-day road trip. "... I think it's something that you just adapt to," Van Slyke said of riding the bus. "When you first get drafted they just throw you right on the bus, and you're on the bus for eight, ten hours and you don't really have time to think about, 'Oh man, this is miserable.'" Photo by Kevin Benedict

BOTTOM LEFT: Scott Van Slyke looks on as pitchers Doug Brooks and Josh Wall, far right, joke around during a card game that also included pitcher Steven Johnson, left, in the away clubhouse prior to a game against the Clinton LumberKings at Alliant Energy Field in Clinton, Iowa. Photo by Kevin Benedict

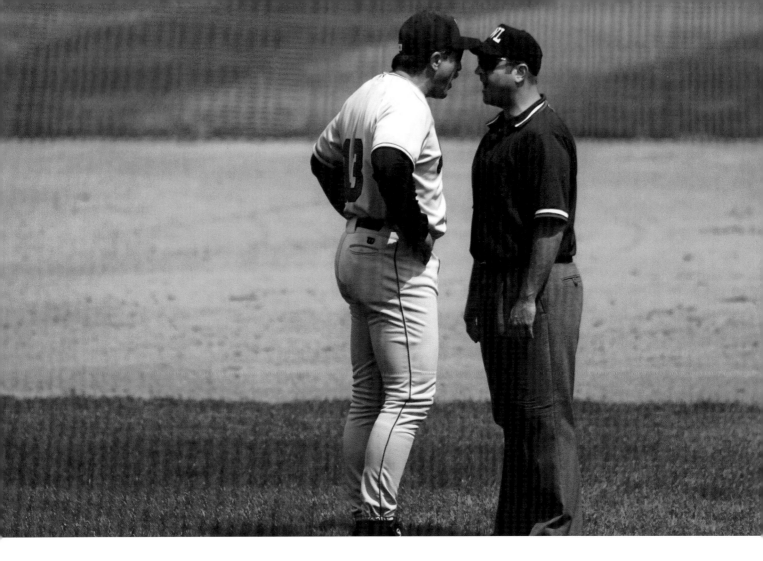

Dodgers Let Parrish Go

By Chris Marchand

Lance Parrish got some bad news from the Los Angeles Dodgers on Wednesday.

Just two days after the Loons completed their inaugural season, the Dodgers informed Parrish that he would not be back to manage the Great Lakes Loons next season. Dodgers' Director of Player Development De Jon Watson indicated to Parrish that the lack of improvement by the team was the reason for his dismissal.

"I talked to De Jon Watson (Tuesday) morning," Parrish said. "He called me to let me know that they were not renewing my contract. He let me know that … he personally wasn't satisfied with the progress that the team had made. We finished close to .500 in the first half and then did not make any progress from that point forward. I guess someone has to be accountable for that, so I'm the logical choice."

The Loons finished the season with a 57-82 mark — the third worst record in the 14-team Midwest League.

The decision came as a shock to Parrish, who was named the Loons' manager last November.

"It took me completely by surprise," Parrish said. "As many roving instructors and front office personnel that have come through Midland, no one ever said anything about our work ethic and things that we need to do differently."

It's the second time that Parrish has been let go by the Dodgers. In 1993, Parrish signed with the Dodgers as a free agent. He never played in a Major League game for the team as the Dodgers opted to go with rookie Mike Piazza at catcher. Parrish played 11 games for the Dodgers' AAA team in Albuquerque before being released.

This time around, Parrish was baffled by the club's decision.

"I'm a little disappointed that I was let go in this fashion," Parrish said. "I thought I had a good relationship with the Dodgers and the people in this organization. I certainly thought they could have handled it a little bit differently. Wherever I fell short as a manager, that's always something that's open for discussion when the season's over. We can change tactics, strategies or work ethic and move forward.

"They chose to sever the ties. I guess they didn't think I did a good enough job and now I'm free to look elsewhere."

The future of the Loons' coaches — hitting coach Garey Ingram and pitching coach Glenn Dishman — is still not known. Both are going to coach this fall in developmental leagues in Arizona.

The Loons began the season as one of the youngest teams in the Midwest League. They featured no less than 10 players under the age of 20. As a result, they struggled early.

ABOVE: Great Lakes Loons manager Lance Parrish argues with an umpire during a game against the Swing of the Quad Cities in Davenport, Iowa. Photo by Kevin Benedict

They were 15-23 on May 17. But the Loons won seven of their final nine games of the first half to build momentum heading into the second half.

But the second half was a different story. First-half standouts Bridger Hunt and Cody White were promoted and the Loons lost eight of their first 10 games in the second half and never recovered.

On top of that, pitching ace Clayton Kershaw and leading hitter Josh Bell were promoted late in the season. The Loons were 23-46 in the second half, including a league-low 11 wins at home.

"It was never stressed to me one way or the other that it was direly important to win," Parrish said. "It was always my understanding that developing players was more important than wins or losses. We knew coming in that we had a young crew and there was work to be done."

"If it was about winning or losing, I thought they would have tried to stack this team more," Parrish said.

The Loons had the highest team earned run average in the Midwest League and also ranked last in defense.

Parrish had planned on coming back next season.

"I was planning on doing whatever the Dodgers wanted me to do," Parrish said. "I tried to state during the last week of the season that I'm an employee of the Dodgers. If they wanted to send

me back to Midland, it would have been great."

Loons' president and general manager Paul Barbeau expressed his disappointment in Parrish's dismissal.

"I want to express how much we appreciate what Lance has meant to the Loons' franchise," Barbeau said. "Lance has been a major part of our franchise in its first year and always will be a major part of our franchise's history. He has been a wonderful representative of the Great Lakes

Loons since the day he became part of our family.

"We were thrilled when the Dodgers announced that Lance Parrish would be the manager for our club in its first year," Barbeau said. "Today, we are disappointed obviously that the relationship between the Loons and Lance is coming to an end." ■

FUN FIGURES

Families, Other Groups Attended, Many From Outside Tri-County Region

GROUP OUTINGS: More than 56,000 people attended games as part of group outings in 2007. Of those, 65 percent were from outside of Midland County. A full 35 percent of those were from outside of Midland, Saginaw and Bay counties.

Ticket Packages

FULL AND HALF SEASON, 24-, 16- AND 8-GAME PLANS: 1,939 businesses or households bought one of these packages in 2007. Of those, 43 percent are from outside of Midland County.

SINGLE-GAME TICKETS: More than 119,000 people bought single-game tickets in 2007. Sixty-two percent are from outside Midland County. Thirty percent are from outside of Midland, Saginaw and Bay counties.

BELOW: Loons right fielder Tommy Giles gazes out of the dugout following his team's 4-3 loss against the Burlington Bees at Dow Diamond. Giles struck out with the bases loaded for the second out in the bottom of the ninth inning, but went 3-5 on the game and scored two runs for the Loons.   Photo by Kevin Benedict

CHAPTER NINE

The Fans

Fans Love the Entertainment
By Fred Kelly

Is a guy who can dance to "YMCA" as important to the Great Lakes Loons' success as a guy who hits .300 and plays good defense?

Maybe not quite. But, according to Paul Barbeau, a guy like that certainly helps.

As the team's general manager, Barbeau is responsible for making sure that fans are entertained before, during, and after the game — and a lot of times, that has nothing to do with baseball.

"(In-game entertainment is) incredibly important," Barbeau said. "A lot of people talked about how we were able to draw fans despite a below-average (win-loss) record. ... Our fans were thrilled with the season as a whole, and part of that was the entertainment value."

It's no secret that entertainment is indeed a

big part of minor league baseball's appeal.

Postgame fireworks.

Promotional games and contests.

Theme nights.

It's all part of making sure that fans have an enjoyable experience at the ballpark — even when the home team isn't winning.

And when you have a lot of repeat business, it is imperative to give fans something new on a regular basis, Barbeau noted.

"Really, the challenge is to keep (the entertainment) fresh and realizing that people come to a lot of different games, and so you have to give them a different show every night," he said.

In the Loons' case, the team has a full-time four-person marketing and promotions staff

ABOVE: Kyle Stoll, 8, of Midland, Matt Baker, 13, of Midland, and Carter Stoll, 11, of Midland, view the fireworks from the outfield at Dow Diamond. Photo by Alex Swawinski

LEFT: Denny Wuolle of Essexville views the Great Lakes Loons game against the Fort Wayne Wizards. "I'll be back next year. I kind of wish they made it to the playoffs. I really have more fun here than a Tigers game," Wuollie said. Photo by Alex Swawinski

ABOVE: Carter Stoll, 11, Matt Baker, 13, and Kyle Stoll, 8, al of Midland, view the fireworks from the outfield of Dow Diamond.   Photo by Alex Stawinski
BELOW: Isaac Morrison, 6, his father, John Morrison, brother, Andrew Morrison, 4, and mother, Karen Morrison, of Midland, view the fireworks after a game at Dow Diamond. "The Loons always win when we come," John Morrison said.   Photo by Alex Stawinski

which generates ideas for home game entertainment. While the marketing staff comes up with some of the ideas themselves, other ideas are borrowed, Barbeau said.

"It's really our staff using experiences we've had in the past, either as employees of a team or (as spectators) at other ballparks," he said.

" ... I'm cursed now," he added with a chuckle. "I don't go to a sporting event just to watch a sporting event anymore. I go and look at everything else in the facility and try to get ideas for our own operation. ... It definitely changes the way you view sporting events."

A lot of times, Barbeau noted, the marketing staff tries to come up with entertainment ideas which have a natural correlation with one of the team's sponsors. For example, the "Science in Baseball" event — in which local high school students participated in a sort of science fair competition with a baseball theme — was sponsored by Dow Corning Corp.

The emphasis was on science education, a natural fit for Dow Corning.

"That's really what drives a lot of (our ideas) — trying to not just put the entertainment out there but also trying to tie it to sponsor objectives and what's a good fit for a sponsor," Barbeau said.

Another promotion that was a natural fit was "Raining Money Night" — during which fans were invited onto the field to round up money dropped from a helicopter — sponsored by Chemical Bank.

Sometimes, Barbeau noted, a particular promotion has little to do with the sponsor's business but is a fun way to get the sponsor some name recognition.

He pointed to Holiday Inn's sponsoring human hamster ball races throughout the season as a good example.

"Human hamster ball races have nothing to do with Holiday Inn or staying at their hotel," Barbeau said. "But it's still a good way to get their name out and put a smile on people's faces."

Among the more popular promotions that the Loons did this year, Barbeau said, were theme nights such as "Halloween Night," "Vegas Night" and "Disco Night." Those games featured staff dressed in costumes, touring performers putting on shows between innings, and superimposing graphics on the players' mugshots on the scoreboard — such as placing "Lance Parrish mustaches" on the players' faces during "Lance Parrish Bobblehead Night."

"Our production team is fantastic at that," Barbeau said of the scoreboard graphics hijinx.

Another hit with fans, Barbeau said, was a promotion in which the Loons dressed in vintage 1950s-era uniforms and entered Dow Diamond through a "cornfield" in the outfield, a la Field of Dreams.

"We really got a good charge throughout the stadium and had people talking about that before and after the event," Barbeau said. "We got a lot of reaction from that one."

Perhaps the most popular promotion, though, was simply lighting off a few fireworks. As Barbeau pointed out, the Loons had fireworks shows after 10 different home games, and all 10 of those games were sell-outs.

"People love fireworks shows, obviously," he said. "That's kind of the minor league baseball staple." ■

ABOVE: Before the start of a game in June, Loons Legends members, from left, Jeanne Pfeiffer, Elaine Zielinski and Pam Spielvogel get the crowd going by chanting, "lets go Loons, lets go." The group's members range in age from late 50s to the early 80s. "They're fun to watch," Lee Smith said after the group filed into the isle of his section shouting chants and punching their fists into the air. Photo by Brett Marshall

ABOVE: Directions for a new chant of Loons Legends. Photo by Brett Marshall

LEFT: Mary Musich, of Larkin Township, fashioned her own Loons headwear from a headband and a stuffed animal she got from the Audubon Society. Photo by Jason Johns

BELOW: Jeanne Pfeiffer, left, covered her face and Jerry Grewe, right, chuckled after Carol Ostergren, center, lost track of a chant while they practiced beneath the stands. The Loons Legends practiced for several months at the Midland Community Center to learn five chants before the group's first public performance in June. Photo by Brett Marshall

Fans Support Loons In a Big Way

By Fred Kelly

The Great Lakes Loons may not have always competed well on the field, but they certainly held their own at the box office.

In their inaugural season, the Loons finished fifth in the Midwest League in total attendance, drawing 324,564 fans to Dow Diamond for an average of 4,773 per home game.

That's a far cry from the team's original projections, which, according to General Manager Paul Barbeau, were 220,000 total and 3,000 per game.

After the season got under way and tickets were going fast, the Loons upped their season projections somewhat but never expected the kind of support they received, Barbeau noted.

"As the momentum started building, we thought maybe we could do 270 or 280 (thousand). ... Then, we started thinking maybe we could hit 300 (thousand), but we kind of crashed right through that," Barbeau said." ... We're

thrilled. That's a big number."

The Loons' final numbers are even more impressive considering that they play in a much smaller ballpark than any of the four teams which finished ahead of them in attendance. They also play in a smaller market than all but one of those teams.

The Dayton Dragons, based in Dayton, Ohio, finished first in the Midwest League, averaging over 8,600 fans per game for a season total of 585,348. The Dragons' Fifth Third Field has a capacity of 7,230, and the team has sold out all home games for seven consecutive seasons.

Dayton is the first and only Minor League Baseball team to sell out every home game before the season has even begun.

"They do a fantastic job (of marketing their team)," Barbeau said of the Dragons." ... They do some pretty amazing things. Those are the kinds of results we strive for."

Kane County, West Michigan and Lansing finished second, third, and fourth, respectively, in attendance this year. The capacity of their stadiums ranges from 7,400 to 11,000, and only Kane County, based in Geneva, Ill., has a smaller population base (19,500) than the Loons. ■

ABOVE: Scott Van Slyke prepares to sign an autograph in a little notebook handed to him by Kara Borucki, 4, of Madison, Alabama, as her father Greg Borucki, second from bottom left, stands nearby before Scott boarded the bus following a game at John O'Donnell Stadium in Davenport, Iowa, on April 30. Greg said he and his daughter were trying to watch all 14 Midwest League teams play during a seven day road trip. "They're the reason we have a job," Van Slyke said of the fans. "If we didn't have fans there would be no baseball." Photo by Kevin Benedict

ABOVE: Mary Musich, left, of Larkin Township and Ruth McPhillips of Midland celebrate as the Great Lakes Loons pull ahead of the South Bend Silver Hawks in the sixth inning. The two women were among the more than 40 fans that traveled by bus and then packed into two suites at Stanley Coveleski Stadium to watch the Loons' first game in history. Photo by Jason Johns

LEFT: Brandon Palley, 5, of Houghton Lake, and Joshua Maze, 10, of St. Helen, have their ticket stubs autographed by a Great Lakes Loon player. Photo by Alex Stawinski

BELOW: Michael Musial, 8, of Alma, is splashed with water upon reaching home base during the running of the bases after the Great Lakes Loons game at Dow Diamond in September. Photo by Alex Stawinski

Booster Club

By John Kennett

Joe Garza knows baseball and speaks Spanish. He was just the kind of person the Great Lakes Loons Booster Club was looking for on Thursday night.

Garza was one of 35 people attending the first ever Loons Booster Club meeting at the Garden Room of the Holiday Inn.

"I'll see what I can do (as far as hosting a player)," said Garza. "I live out here on Wixom (Lake) and retired recently."

The Loons' goal, according to Loons' President Paul Barbeau, is to get every Loons' player paired up with a host family. The team is especially looking for Spanish-speaking families, as some of the Loons' players may be native Spanish speakers.

Having coached summer league college baseball players and being fluent in Spanish, Garza recognizes the struggles that the Spanish-speaking players may experience.

"I know that there are going to be a lot of

ABOVE: Great Lakes Loons right fielder Scott Van Slyke greeted children as they filed past the visitors dugout prior to a game against the Swing of the Quad Cities in Davenport, Iowa, on May 2, 2007. Photo by Kevin Benedict.

BELOW: Fourth and fifth grade students from Chestnut Hill Elementary give Loons players Francisco Felix, left, and Francisco Lizarraga bunny ears while posing for a group picture in the school gymnasium. Felix and Lizarraga, both from Mexico, visited the school to interact with the students in Spanish. Photo by Brett Marshall

ballplayers that are going to be handicapped with that language barrier," said Garza.

Jim Wright, booster club president, was pleased with the turnout at Thursday's meeting.

"Generally, I think that the people are very excited," said Wright. "I think for an organizational meeting (it was well-attended). It really wasn't a meeting to sign up members. The people who came here are the people who are truly interested in working on committees and being on the boards."

The mission statement of the club is to "be enthusiastically supportive of players and team personnel and their families, making their stay in Midland a great experience whether it be vocally rooting at games or providing special needs for the players to help make Midland feel like home."

The booster club, which is a separate organization from the Loons, plans to provide different areas of support for the players.

The club has formed committees to help out in the areas of membership, welcome, communications (website/newsletter), road trip/snacks, and host homes.

Janna Luebkert experienced first-hand what a minor league baseball team can do for a downtown. Before moving to Midland, she interned for the management facility that owned Oldsmobile Park, home of the Lansing Lugnuts.

"(The Lugnuts) did a lot of great things for Lansing," said Luebkert. "I know what (a team) can do for a community.

"It brought a lot of people back downtown, especially families and young people," added Luebkert, who lived in Venezuela for three years and speaks fluent Spanish.

Luebkert signed on to be part of the welcoming committee.

The next step for the booster club is to take all the applications received Thursday and start asking people to serve on committees.

"We're going to start calling people and saying, 'This is what we need. Can you do it for us?'" said Wright.

Wright said he has had as many e-mails from interested people as people that showed up at the meeting.

Booster club members will get the opportunity to establish relationships with the players, according to Wright. But members will not receive discounts for Loons' games.. ■

ABOVE: Great Lakes Loons pitchers Arismendy Castillo, center left, of the Dominican Republic, and Jesus Rodriguez, of Mexico, center right, joke with Dow High advanced placement Spanish students Ricky Gulotti, 17, Neal Rakesh, 17, and Samantha Greenberg, 18, in the team's clubhouse at Dow Diamond. Connie Blanchard's purpose in taking her students to meet the players was to both welcome the players to town, but to also have her students work on their conversational Spanish. Photo by Brett Marshall

ABOVE: Great Lakes Loons pitcher Christopher Malone autographs Preston Eurich, 9, of Sebewaing's hat while his brother Connor Eurick, 11, right, watches before a game at Dow Diamond in August. "It is pretty cool that you don't have to have a special pass to get autographs," Connor Eurick said. Photo by Alex Stawinski

RIGHT: Frances Longsdorf and husband, Charles Longsdorf, of Midland, cheer on the Great Lakes Loons. It was the couple's first outing to Dow Diamond. Photo by Alex Stawinski

PREVIOUS PAGE: From left, Brandon Quider, 12, Elizabeth Martin, 11, Julia Tisdale, 12, and Madie Mulder, 12, dance in dwindling rain to music at Dow Diamond during a nearly two hour delay that occurred in Wednesday's game between the Loons and the Wisconsin Timber Rattlers due to a storm that passed through the area. Photo by Kevin Benedict

LEFT: Couples Jesse and Brian Armstrong of Saginaw and Joanna and John Evans of Midland watch the Great Lakes Loons against the South Bend Silver Hawks. Photo by Alex Stawinski

BELOW: Sheila Goschke, of Estey, left, poses for a picture with Lou E. Loon as Goschke's father-in-law, LaVerne Goschke, 84, of Saginaw, looks on during an event at which "Dow Diamond" was announced as the name of the baseball stadium in Midland. Photo by Kevin Benedict

RIGHT: Ryan Eastman and his son Dylan, 4, watch as T-shirts are launched from the stage after the unveiling of the name, the Great Lakes Loons. "It's different than I thought it would be. The Great Lakes thing is cool," Ryan said of the new name.   Photo by Brett Marshall

Game-by-Game Stats

Date	Opponent	Result	Record	Winner	Loser	Save	Time	Att
April 5	@South Bend	W 10-3	1-0	Doug Brooks	Brett Anderson	None	2:52	989
April 6	@South Bend	W 3-1	2-0	Michael Gardner	Craig Pfautz	Jesus Rodriguez	2:43	628
April 9	@Fort Wayne	L 1-0	2-1	Nathan Culp	Cody White	R.J. Rodriguez	2:19	1753
April 10	@Fort Wayne	W 3-2	3-1	Michael Gardner	Aaron Breit	Francisco Felix	2:31	943
April 12	@Fort Wayne (1)	L 9-3 (7)	3-2	Andrew Underwood	Josh Wall	None	2:04	N/A
April 12	@Fort Wayne (2)	W 5-2 (7)	4-2	Clayton Kershaw	Orlando Lara	None	1:53	3280
April 13	Lansing	L 6-2	4-3	A.J. Wideman	Steven Johnson	None	2:55	5454
April 14	Lansing	L 2-0	4-4	Chase Lirette	Cody White	Paul Phillips	2:31	5494
April 15	@Lansing	L 3-1	4-5	Benjamin Harrison	Doug Brooks	Seth Overbey	2:18	1612
April 16	@Lansing	L 5-4	4-6	Nathan Starner	Francisco Felix	Seth Overbey	2:22	1117
April 17	Peoria	L 4-2	4-7	Billy Muldowney	Josh Wall	Rocky Roquet	2:45	2242
April 19	Peoria (1)	L 2-1 (7)	4-8	Alessandro Maestri	Doug Brooks	None	1:58	N/A
April 19	Peoria (2)	L 6-1 (7)	4-9	Rafael Dolis	Steven Johnson	None	2:03	3190
April 20	Peoria	L 3-0	4-10	Jose Ceda	Cody White	Rocky Roquet	2:42	4340
April 21	Cedar Rapids	W 5-4	5-10	Francisco Felix	Jeremy Haynes	Miguel Sanfler	2:51	5382
April 22	Cedar Rapids	W 10-1	6-10	Josh Wall	Sean OSullivan	None	2:33	4567
April 23	Cedar Rapids	L 5-0	6-11	Tim Schoeninger	Michael Gardner	None	2:29	1851
April 24	Cedar Rapids	W 2-1	7-11	Garrett White	Robert Romero	None	2:22	3633
April 27	@Clinton (1)	W 4-2 (7)	8-11	Steven Johnson	Glenn Swanson	Garrett White	2:04	N/A
April 27	@Clinton (2)	W 7-4	9-11	Miguel Ramirez	Brennan Garr	Doug Brooks	2:52	4521
April 28	@Clinton	W 11-9	10-11	Michael Gardner	Timothy Gudex	None	2:50	1837
April 29	@Clinton	L 5-3	10-12	Michael Ballard	Josh Wall	Brett Zamzow	2:39	4596
April 30	@Quad Cities	W 1-0	11-12	Clayton Kershaw	Brad Furnish	Miguel Ramirez	2:34	1731
May 1	@Quad Cities	L 4-2	11-13	Michael Schellinger	Garrett White	None	2:27	892
May 2	@Quad Cities	L 13-6	11-14	Brandon Dickson	Cody White	None	2:59	3904
May 3	@Quad Cities	L 3-0	11-15	P.J. Walters	Thomas Melgarejo	Kenneth Maiques	2:14	1202
May 4	Beloit	L 6-3	11-16	Adam Hawes	Josh Wall	Aaron Craig	2:23	5434
May 5	Beloit	L 8-1	11-17	Jeff Manship	Michael Gardner	None	2:29	4746
May 6	Beloit	L 7-6	11-18	Danny Vais	Arismendy Castillo	Robert Delaney	2:59	5114
May 7	Beloit	W 4-0	12-18	Cody White	Jose Lugo	None	1:59	5427
May 8	Wisconsin	W 5-3	13-18	Clayton Kershaw	Steven Richard	Jesus Rodriguez	2:23	2533
May 9	Wisconsin	L 6-4	13-19	Joseph Kantakevich	Miguel Sanfler	Andrew Barb	2:52	2268
May 10	Wisconsin	L 4-2	13-20	Natividad Dilone	Garrett White	Andrew Barb	2:48	3822
May 11	Wisconsin	W 6-5	14-20	Miguel Ramirez	Rollie Gibson	None	2:48	5441
May 12	@West Michigan	W 3-2	15-20	Cody White	Christopher Cody	Jesus Rodriguez	2:18	7562
May 13	@West Michigan	L 12-5	15-21	Jonah Nickerson	Clayton Kershaw	Jeffrey Gerbe	2:32	5357
May 14	West Michigan	L 5-4	15-22	Lauren Gagnier	Thomas Melgarejo	Brett Jensen	2:30	3233
May 17	@Kane County	L 6-3	15-23	James Heuser	Josh Wall	None	2:44	4071
May 18	@Kane County	W 9-2	16-23	Cody White	John Herrera	None	3:00	6379
May 19	@Kane County	W 3-0	17-23	Clayton Kershaw	Henry A. Rodriguez	Joe Jones	2:49	6629
May 20	@Kane County	L 6-3	17-24	Scott Deal	Thomas Melgarejo	Scott Moore	2:29	5808
May 21	@Burlington	W 7-4	18-24	Arismendy Castillo	Brent Fisher	Miguel Ramirez	2:35	1002
May 22	@Burlington	W 10-7	19-24	Josh Wall	Everett Teaford	Garrett White	2:37	487
May 23	@Burlington	L 4-2	19-25	Matt Campbell	Cody White	Mario Santiago	2:31	566
May 24	@Burlington	L 3-2	19-26	Harold Mozingo	Clayton Kershaw	Tyler Chambliss	2:32	410
May 25	@Lansing	W 13-6	20-26	Jesus Rodriguez	Kyle Ginley	None	3:00	5138
May 26	@Lansing	L 10-3	20-27	Reidier Gonzalez	Arismendy Castillo	Julio Pinto	2:38	4993

Date	Opponent	Result	Record	Winner	Loser	Save	Time	Att
May 27	Lansing	L 10-5	20-28	Chase Lirette	Josh Wall	Adrian Martin	3:02	5531
May 28	Lansing	W 8-6	21-28	Cody White	Edward Rodriguez	Miguel Ramirez	2:50	4540
May 29	Dayton	W 3-1	22-28	Clayton Kershaw	Daniel Guerrero	Miguel Ramirez	2:31	2128
May 30	Dayton	L 7-5	22-29	Rafael Gonzalez	Thomas Melgarejo	Jose Rojas	2:39	4041
May 31	Dayton	W 7-6	23-29	Miguel Sanfler	Ramon Geronimo	None	2:35	3269
June 1	Dayton	L 5-2	23-30	Sean Watson	Josh Wall	Jose Rojas	2:37	5327
June 2	@South Bend (1)	W 6-3 (7)	24-30	Cody White	Jordan Norberto	None	1:55	N/A
June 2	@South Bend (2)	L 3-0 (7)	24-31	Derik Nippert	Michael Gardner	Reid Mahon	1:54	2174
June 3	@South Bend	W 10-9	25-31	Clayton Kershaw	Eddie Romero	Miguel Ramirez	2:58	1535
June 4	@South Bend	W 11-9	26-31	Thomas Melgarejo	Tony Barnette	Doug Brooks	3:08	2546
June 5	@South Bend	L 12-2	26-32	Brett Anderson	Arismendy Castillo	None	2:47	1481
June 7	Fort Wayne	W 6-4	27-32	Cody White	Ernesto Frieri	Miguel Ramirez	3:07	3589
June 8	Fort Wayne	L 5-3	27-33	Andrew Underwood	Garrett White	R.J. Rodriguez	2:33	5677
June 9	Fort Wayne	L 5-4	27-34	Derek McDaid	Thomas Melgarejo	R.J. Rodriguez	2:46	5110
June 10	Fort Wayne	W 8-5	28-34	Miguel Sanfler	Grant Varnell	None	2:51	5024
June 11	@West Michigan (1)	W 5-4 (7)	29-34	Josh Wall	Jonah Nickerson	Miguel Ramirez	2:03	N/A
June 11	@West Michigan (2)	W 3-0 (7)	30-34	David Pfeiffer	Lauren Gagnier	Michael Gardner	2:06	6057
June 12	@West Michigan	W 9-7	31-34	Cody White	Angel Castro	Miguel Sanfler	3:01	6340
June 13	Lansing	W 7-3	32-34	Clayton Kershaw	Graham Godfrey	None	2:27	5034
June 14	Lansing	L 8-2	32-35	Kyle Ginley	Garrett White	None	2:50	4941
June 15	South Bend	W 7-2	33-35	Arismendy Castillo	Tony Barnette	None	2:19	5052
June 16	South Bend	W 7-4	34-35	Josh Wall	Brett Anderson	David Pfeiffer	2:55	4947
June 17	South Bend	L 4-3	34-36	Cesar Valdez	Miguel Sanfler	Reid Mahon	2:35	5230
				End First half				
June 21	South Bend	L 11-5	34-37	Jordan Norberto	Arismendy Castillo	Mark Romanczuk	3:15	5012
June 22	South Bend	L 3-0	34-38	Derik Nippert	Josh Wall	Reid Mahon	2:37	5612
June 23	South Bend	L 3-2	34-39	Eddie Romero	Matt Gomez de Segura	Jorge Perez	2:31	5213
June 24	South Bend	W 2-1	35-39	Cody White	Cesar Valdez	Thomas Melgarejo	2:05	5181
June 25	@Fort Wayne	L 3-2	35-40	R.J. Rodriguez	Matt Gomez de Segura	None	2:30	4745
June 27	@Fort Wayne (1)	L 1-0 (7)	35-41	Steve Delabar	Josh Wall	R.J. Rodriguez	1:28	N/A
June 27	@Fort Wayne (2)	L 6-0 (7)	35-42	Stephen Faris	Steven Johnson	None	1:47	1578
June 28	@Fort Wayne	W 6-4	36-42	Christopher Malone	Andrew Underwood	Thomas Melgarejo	2:46	2692
June 29	Lansing	L 15-7	36-43	Zachary Dials	Clayton Kershaw	None	3:04	5746
June 30	Lansing	L 2-1	36-44	Nathan Starner	Arismendy Castillo	Adrian Martin	2:52	5792
July 1	Lansing	W 6-1	37-44	Thomas Melgarejo	Graham Godfrey	Miguel Sanfler	2:44	5037
July 2	Lansing	W 7-6	38-44	David Pfeiffer	Benjamin Harrison	Miguel Ramirez	2:57	4833
July 3	@ Dayton	L 18-2	38-45	Travis Webb	Steven Johnson	None	3:05	8725
July 4	@Dayton	W 5-0	39-45	Thomas Melgarejo	Mike Stanton	None	2:57	8870
July 5	@Dayton	L 20-3	39-46	Rafael Gonzalez	Arismendy Castillo	None	3:26	8259
July 6	@Dayton	L 8-2	39-47	Jordan Smith	David Pfeiffer	None	2:30	8379
July 7	@West Michigan	W 4-1	40-47	Josh Wall	Lauren Gagnier	Miguel Ramirez	2:28	8563
July 8	@West Michigan	L 9-4	40-48	Luis Marte	Steven Johnson	None	2:29	4077
July 9	@West Michigan	W 8-6	41-48	Paul Coleman	Matt OBrien	Miguel Ramirez	3:12	3520
July 13	Burlington	W 6-5 (10)	42-48	Thomas Melgarejo	Aaron Hartsock	None	3:15	5795
July 14	Burlington	L 6-5 (11)	42-49	Ryan DiPietro	Miguel Sanfler	Chris Hayes	3:21	5488
July 15	Burlington	L 7-5	42-50	Aaron Hartsock	David Pfeiffer	None	3:09	5663
July 16	Burlington	L 4-3	42-51	Henry Barrera	Miguel Sanfler	Jim Wladyka	3:12	3633
July 17	Quad Cities	L 13-7	42-52	Michael Schellinger	Paul Coleman	None	3:04	4228
July 18	Quad Cities	W 10-4 (7)	43-52	David Pfeiffer	Tyler Herron	None	2:04	4549
July 19	Quad Cities	L 4-3	43-53	Kyle Sadowski	Clayton Kershaw	Kenneth Maiques	2:42	5742
July 20	Quad Cities	L 6-2	43-54	Marco Gonzalez	Joe Jones	None	2:52	5626
July 21	@Beloit	L 8-3	43-55	Alex Burnett	James Adkins	None	2:41	3003
July 22	@Beloit	W 6-4	44-55	David Pfeiffer	Jesus Carnevales	Miguel Ramirez	3:10	2225

Date	Opponent	Result	Record	Winner	Loser	Save	Time	Att
July 23	@Beloit	L 7-6 (10)	44-56	Anthony Slama	Thomas Melgarejo	None	3:20	831
July 24	@Beloit	L 12-11 (12)	44-57	Jesus Carnevales	James Peterson	None	4:19	1807
July 26	@Wisconsin	W 4-3	45-57	Blake Brannon	Joseph Kantakevich	Miguel Ramirez	2:56	4024
July 27	@Wisconsin	L 5-2	45-58	Michael Wagner	Arismendy Castillo	None	2:25	3515
July 28	@Wisconsin	L 4-3 (7)	45-59	Rollie Gibson	Joe Jones	None	2:17	3777
July 29	@Wisconsin	W 8-5	46-59	Steven Johnson	Nolan Gallagher	Miguel Ramirez	3:00	2487
July 30	Clinton	L 8-3	46-60	Jeremiah Harr	Clayton Kershaw	Anton Maxwell	2:46	4541
July 31	Clinton	W 9-8 (10)	47-60	Blake Brannon	John Slusarz	None	3:12	4692
August 1	Clinton	L 5-3	47-61	Kasey Kiker	Arismendy Castillo	Joshua Lueke	2:50	4564
August 2	Clinton	L 8-1	47-62	Omar Poveda	Paul Coleman	None	2:45	4337
August 3	Kane County	L 8-1	47-63	Trevor Cahill	Thomas Melgarejo	None	2:58	5623
August 4	Kane County	L 7-4	47-64	Eric Sheridan	Blake Brannon	None	3:33	5765
August 5	Kane County	L 11-2	47-65	James Heuser	Christopher Malone	None	3:01	5346
August 6	Kane County	W 10-6	48-65	Arismendy Castillo	Jason Fernandez	None	3:25	4213
August 7	@Peoria	W 10-2	49-65	Paul Coleman	Robert Hernandez	None	2:56	3047
August 8	@Peoria	L 3-1	49-66	Casey Lambert	Thomas Melgarejo	Alessandro Maestri	2:22	2394
August 9	@Peoria	L 5-4	49-67	Alessandro Maestri	Miguel Ramirez	None	2:53	3067
August 10	@Peoria	L 14-3	49-68	Jacob Renshaw	Kyle Smit	None	2:59	6673
August 11	@Cedar Rapids	W 3-2	50-68	Timothy Sexton	Thomas Mendoza	Miguel Ramirez	2:45	3828
August 12	@Cedar Rapids	L 8-4	50-69	David Herndon	Paul Coleman	Warner A. Madrigal	2:33	2923
August 13	@Cedar Rapids	W 3-2	51-69	Steven Johnson	Amalio Diaz	Thomas Melgarejo	2:14	1801
August 14	@Cedar Rapids	L 5-3	52-69	Josh Wall	Jeremy Haynes	Miguel Ramirez	2:53	2587
August 16	Dayton	L 6-1	52-70	Travis Webb	Kyle Smit	None	2:19	5594
August 17	Dayton	L 13-8 (10)	52-71	Ramon Geronimo	Christopher Malone	None	3:56	5675
August 18	@South Bend	L 9-1	52-72	Chad Beck	Paul Coleman	None	2:26	2296
August 19	@South Bend			Cancelled - Rain				
August 20	West Michigan	W 2-1	53-72	Joe Jones	Dan Fyvie	Josh Wall	2:29	4750
August 21	West Michigan	L 6-1	53-73	Charles Furbish	Kyle Smit	None	2:06	5159
August 22	West Michigan	W 9-2	54-73	Timothy Sexton	Jonah Nickerson	None	2:28	5404
August 23	West Michigan	L 4-0	54-74	Duane Below	Paul Coleman	Casey Fien	2:45	5318
August 24	@Lansing	L 4-1	54-75	Julio Pinto	Christopher Malone	Po-Hsuan Keng	2:17	7102
August 25	@Lansing	L 6-2	54-76	Chris Reddout	Josh Wall	Edgar Estanga	2:47	8103
August 26	@Lansing	L 8-7	54-77	Ron Lowe	Steven Johnson	Po-Hsuan Keng	2:39	5102
August 27	@Lansing	L 7-4	54-78	Kyle Ginley	Kyle Smit	Edgar Estanga	2:21	1541
August 28	South Bend	W 2-1	55-78	Timothy Sexton	Eddie Romero	Christopher Malone	2:34	5455
August 29	South Bend	W 7-5	56-78	Jonathon Figueroa	Mark Romanczuk	Thomas Melgarejo	2:45	5029
August 30	@West Michigan	L 4-2	56-79	Phil Napolitan	Joe Jones	Luis Marte	2:43	4872
August 31	@West Michigan	W 5-3 (10)	57-79	Miguel Sanfler	Zachary Piccola	None	2:38	9213
September 1	Fort Wayne	L 11-2 (7)	57-80	Brandon Gomes	Kyle Smit	None	2:15	5339
September 2	Fort Wayne	L 8-3	57-81	Brent Carter	Timothy Sexton	None	2:28	5484
September 3	Fort Wayne	L 6-2	57-82	Dylan Axelrod	Blake Brannon	Rolando Valdez	2:57	5515

Batting (alphabetical)

Player	GP	R	H	HR	RBI	Ave.
Juan Apodaca	58	23	53	8	27	.259
Josh Bell	108	65	115	15	62	.289
Matt Berezay	116	58	118	13	64	.276
Parker Brooks	6	1	1	0	1	.071
Justin Fuller	29	13	21	1	3	.239
Thomas Giles	34	24	40	6	18	.320
Adolfo Gonzalez	84	42	93	5	29	.296
Elian Herrara	9	3	6	0	3	.167
Bridger Hunt	46	29	53	1	19	.246
Kenley Jansen	20	5	6	1	6	.102
Francisco Lizarraga	79	35	74	6	29	.261
Brian Mathews	23	8	29	1	2	.319
Preston Mattingly	107	42	85	3	40	.210
Eduardo Perez	116	56	139	14	60	.311
James Peterson	60	20	57	3	28	.271
Michael Rivera	6	2	4	0	2	.211
Juan Rivera	39	20	36	4	16	.252
Trayvon Robinson	110	50	100	2	31	.253
Carlos Santana	86	32	65	7	36	.223
David Sutherland	34	8	23	1	11	.197
Rick Taloa	21	8	16	1	6	.205
Scott Van Slyke	104	38	89	2	35	.254

Pitching (alphabetical)

Player	W-L	G	SV	IP	ER	BB	K	ERA
James Adkins	1-0	11	0	26.0	7	10	30	2.42
Blake Brannon	2-2	13	0	16.1	16	11	13	8.82
Doug Brooks	1-2	13	2	27	17	11	20	5.67
Arismendy Castillo	3-8	23	0	92.1	55	61	67	5.36
Paul Coleman	2-5	11	0	54.2	31	21	29	5.10
Jose Diaz	0-0	2	0	1.1	1	3	0	6.75
Francisco Felix	1-1	10	1	35.1	3	9	35	0.76
Jonathan Figueroa	1-0	5	0	10	1	9	17	0.90
Michael Gardner	3-3	16	1	47	31	12	30	5.94
Yulkin German	0-0	12	0	16	31	21	12	17.44
Matt Segura de Gomez	0-2	8	0	12.1	13	17	13	9.49
Adolfo Gonzalez	0-0	1	0	0.0	0	0	0	0.00
Steven Johnson	3-6	18	0	81.2	44	40	65	4.85
Joe Jones	1-3	26	1	58.1	35	32	42	5.40
Clayton Kershaw	7-5	20	0	97.1	30	50	134	2.77
Christopher Malone	1-3	14	1	39	25	23	41	5.77
Thomas Melgarejo	4-8	33	4	90	62	44	57	6.20
James Peterson	0-1	3	0	2.0	6	5	3	27.00
David Pfeiffer	4-2	12	1	36.2	13	24	19	3.19
Miguel Ramirez	2-1	41	15	51.2	9	30	56	1.57
Jesus Rodriguez	1-0	14	3	31.1	8	7	21	2.30
Miguel Sanfler	3-4	43	3	70	40	63	67	5.14
Timothy Sexton	3-1	5	0	22.2	9	5	25	3.57
Kyle Smit	0-5	5	0	22.2	21	12	26	8.34
Josh Wall	6-10	26	1	129.1	60	48	103	4.18
Cody White	8-5	15	0	76.1	21	41	63	2.48
Garrett White	1-4	23	2	51.1	19	15	63	3.33

Opening Day Roster

JOSH BELL

MATT BEREZAY

DOUG BROOKS

PARKER BROOKS

GLENN DISHMAN

FRANCISCO FELIX

JOE FOX

JUSTIN FULLER

MICHAEL GARDNER

BRIDGER HUNT

GAREY INGRAM

KENLEY JANSEN

Opening Day Roster (cont.)

STEVE JOHNSON

JOE JONES

CLAYTON KERSHAW

FRANCISCO LIZARRAGA

PRESTON MATTINGLY

THOMAS MELGAREJO

LANCE PARRISH

EDUARDO PEREZ

MIGUEL RAMIREZ

MICHAEL RIVERA

TRAYVON ROBINSON

JESUS RODRIGUEZ

Opening Day Roster (cont.)

MIGUEL SANFLER

CARLOS SANTANA

DAVID SUTHERLAND

SCOTT VANSLYKE

JOSH WALL

CODY WHITE

GARRETT WHITE